P9-DHE-807

Richard P. Olson

Joe H. Leonard, Jr.

A NEW DAY
FOR FAMILY
MINISTRY

AN ALBAN INSTITUTE PUBLICATION

The authors and The Alban Institute gratefully acknowledge permission to reprint excerpts from

Children at Risk by James Dobson. Reprinted by permission of Word Publishing. Dallas, TX.

Diversity in American Families by Maxine Baca Zinn. Copyright © 1987 by Harper & Row, Publishers, Inc. Reprinted with permission of HarperCollins Publishers Inc., New York, NY.

Embattled Paradise: The American Family in an Age of Uncertainty by Arlene Skolnick. Copyright © 1991 by Arlene Skolnick. Reprinted with permission of HarperCollins Publishers Inc., New York, NY.

Families at the Crossroads by Rodney Clapp. Copyright © 1993 by Rodney Clapp. Used by permission of InterVarsity Press, P.O. Box 1400, Downers Grove, IL 60515.

The Future of the American Family by George Barna. Reprinted by permission of Moody Press, Chicago, IL.

"Leave No Child Behind" by Marion Wright Edelman, *Church and Society Magazine* 84, no. 2, Presbyterian Church (USA) November-December 1993.

"New Realities of the American Family," *Population Bulletin* 47, No. 2. Reprinted by permission of Population Reference Bureau, Washington, DC.

Normal Family Processes, Second Edition by Froma Walsh, ed., 1993. Reprinted by permission of The Guilford Press, New York, NY.

Old Loyalties, New Ties: Therapeutic Strategies by Emily B. Visher and John S. Visher. Reprinted with permission of Brunner/Mazel, Inc., New York, NY.

"Strengthening Families and Churches in Turbulent Times" by Diana Garland. Reprinted by permission of *Journal of Family Ministry*, Vol. 9, Number 1, Louisville, KY: Gheens Center for Christian Family Ministry, 1995.

"What is a Christian Family?" by Willie S. Teague. Reprinted from *Weavings*, 3, No. 1 (January/February 1988): 27, 31.

The Publications Program of The Alban Institute is assisted by a grant from Trinity Church, New York City.

Library of Congress Catalog Card Number 95-83895
ISBN #1-56699-166-8

CONTENTS

Introduction   v

Chapter 1   Clarifying a Controversy   1

Chapter 2   What Are Families Coming to Anyway?   23
               Families in the Nineties and Beyond

Chapter 3   A Christian Theological-Ethical Response   45

Chapter 4   Supporting Families in the Congregation   64

Chapter 5   Challenges for Family Ministry   103

A Closing Word of Encouragement and Hope   143

Notes   145

Resources   153

90650

INTRODUCTION

Both of us, Dick Olson and Joe Leonard, have had life-long interests and career commitments to understanding and strengthening families. As a matter of fact, it was these commitments that occasioned our meeting each other, coming to enjoy and respect each other, and, eventually, collaborating on projects such as this.

Shortly we will look at the accelerating change in the world of families. Before we do that, however, perhaps we should tell you a little about ourselves and our families. We will communicate better if you know where we are coming from.

Dick was a Depression baby, the second of two children born to a clergyman and spouse in western South Dakota. His father died when Dick was nine, and his family experienced the financial struggle common to many single-parent families. About a year after his father's death, a new minister arrived—a single woman, who with a female friend headed a household of adopted and foster children. Gradually Dick's mother and these two women pooled resources and offered material and emotional support to one another. And so the two families drew together in many ways. (Come to think of it, this conglomerate of people rather resembled the broad definition of family we propose in chapter 2.)

With scholarship aid, Dick was able to attend a church-related liberal arts college and then theological school. Though he did not know it at the time, he married at the statistically precise moment for his era—the fifties. He was twenty-three; Mary Ann was twenty. Two-and-a-half years later, they began their rather typical family of three children. As these children grew to young adulthood, he was exposed to changing mores, particularly as regards nonmarital cohabitation. Eventually each of the three fulfilled their family and cultural script of education (graduate degrees), careers, and marriage—and parenthood for two of the three.

Dick has been a pastor in local church settings for more than thirty-five years. He has served in South Dakota, Wisconsin, Massachusetts, Colorado, and Kansas. In attempting to keep abreast of family needs, he gained further graduate education and pastoral counseling credentials. Two of his pastorates have been interethnic congregations that have included interracial couples. In one setting there was a pressing need for caring response to people seeking remarriage, due to the rigidity of some other churches in that community. In yet another he had to come to grips and give leadership in the face of sexual abuse of children by a church leader. His premarital and marital counseling and marriage enrichment workshops have kept him in touch with the changing and the enduring in folks' marriage aspirations and needs.

Joe was born in 1940 to parents who were the oldest children in their families and had delayed marriage while supporting their mothers and younger siblings. Joe's mother was a career woman who upon marrying his father became a partner in his business. Joe's father owned and operated an auto and truck repair business in Los Angeles and after World War II became a contractor and real estate developer in the southern California desert. Joe and his younger sister grew up in a small resort town with a population that doubled during the winter. Extended family on Joe's father's side trekked to the desert every Thanksgiving for a family feast that usually brought together some eighteen people and sometimes as many as twenty-five.

Joe attended a secular university in California and there met Virginia. They courted for most of three years and married in 1962 following graduation. Both entered graduate school on the east coast and both earned theological degrees. Following graduation and a move to upstate New York and Joe's first full-time pastoral assignment, Matthew was born, followed in three years by Rebecca. Both children have autism, a severe life-long developmental disability, and that fact has markedly shaped the Leonards' experience of "family."

After seven years in an upstate New York university town, Joe and Ginny realized they needed to be in an urban center to find services for their children. They moved to Philadelphia. Joe was called to the national staff of the American Baptist Board of Educational Ministries. There he worked on issues of family ministry, church education administration,

and adult education. His participation in the Commission on Family
Ministries and Human Sexuality of the National Council of Churches
gave him opportunity to explore family issues across many denominations in North America with exposure to global developments in family
education and advocacy. In 1989 he became director of the commission
and currently is engaged full-time in ecumenical work.

Some seven years ago we collaborated on a book about changes in
families. It was eventually published by The Westminster/John Knox
Press under the title *Ministry with Families in Flux* and has been well
received. Readers wanting more detailed analysis and ministry suggestions for many of the family types we discuss may want to look at it.

But time has moved on since that book. And so we write again on
ministry with changing American families. Some of the changes in
society and economy we noted in our previous book have accelerated
and impacted families even more. Others we did not formerly note are
coming into view. We speak of these formidable changes in chapter 1,
where we acknowledge that families not only absorb change, but also
contribute to it and enter into the cultural dialogue.

In chapter 2 we explore the developing landscape of family forms.
We also note the signs of stress in families—and report indications of
their resilience.

While there have been prominent voices from the Christian right
exploring these issues and calling for a return to the standards and practices of an earlier time, we feel that there are alternatives to this view.
No one owns "the" Christian point of view on these matters. And so in
chapter 3 we turn to discerning biblical theologians of the family, and we
outline some possible alternate interpretations. From this, we suggest
perspectives on the ethical decisions facing those who minister with
families today.

Then in chapters 4 and 5 we draw this contemporary and biblical-
theological data into dialogue to create a new paradigm for family ministry. We explore five basic dimensions of family ministry—areas of
enduring concern that should be emphasized whatever the current situation of families.

We go on to list and discuss seven challenges that face leaders
ministering to families in our current milieu. Some of these are thorny
and controversial! With each of these items we offer: discussion of the
issue, implications for ministry, and practical suggestions to help readers
respond.

Discussion questions for each chapter can be found in the closing epilogue.

Families are both a great resource to the church's ministry and in great need of the church's ministry. There are tremendous stresses and changes in families. Business as usual simply will not do.

And so we sketch a road map that will take us to a new day in family ministry.

CHAPTER 1

Clarifying a Controversy

It is my conviction that religious congregations are the most important carriers of meaning that we have, with one exception. They are the most important ground of purpose and direction that we have, with one exception. They are the most important source of an essential element of life—human community—with one exception.

That one exception is the human family.

— Loren Mead[1]

Students of family life agree on at least two things. One point of agreement is the importance of families.

Sociologists note that from time immemorial families have filled the functions and tasks of mutual care and of bearing and guiding the next generation. Sociologists note with alarm the increasing failure of families to fulfill these tasks.

Family therapists and other counselors are aware of the ways families both hurt and heal their individual members; they observe that for individual growth to occur, there needs to be corresponding change and growth in that individual's family.

Theologians point to the tremendous power God has entrusted to human relationships, particularly to intimate partnerships and families. Families are significant in keeping covenant with God and with contributing to the covenant's continuity from generation to generation. They do this by how they guide and discipline and by what they teach, model, and encourage.

Yes, families are important.

The second point of agreement is that families are undergoing great change. We will map out the extent of this change in chapter 2.

At this point, agreement ends. There is widespread controversy over what such change means. Is "the family as an institution" disintegrating, or is it adapting and regrouping?

Is "family decline" responsible for some of the ills of society, such as decreasing school achievement and dropouts, gangs, increased use of drugs, nonmarital pregnancies, unemployment? Or are families simply the recipient of societal and economic changes, the units that feel the painful impact of fluctuations elsewhere?

Should one be hopeful or despairing over the future of American families? Is the Christian leader called to adapt to changing family forms and styles? Or are leaders called to work for deep and systemic change of both the culture and of the patterns of contemporary family life? What do the Bible and Christian faith say to the changing patterns of family life? How is the church to understand the current family scene, and how is it to minister to real families? Such is the maze through which we will attempt to walk in these pages. We are convinced a new paradigm for understanding families and for ministry to/with/on behalf of families is needed.

Families and Culture

Consider the insights of Monica McGoldrick: "Culture . . . is not a monologue, but a dialogue." She points out that families do not develop their rules, beliefs, and rituals in a vacuum. All of this is transmitted from a wider cultural context. Therefore, "No matter what your family background is, it is multicultural. All marriages are to a degree inter-marriages." Each family is not only multicultural, but it is also a collection of immigrants—on the move. We move from the traditions of our ancestors through the world we inhabit to that place the generations after us will occupy.[2]

Throughout history families have interacted with the culture of the day. Of course society and culture have many aspects, including the great variety of people we encounter; the ways of making a livelihood; the economic conditions; the developing technology; the government and military conditions; and the various religious and values systems that undergird society. All aspects of culture affect families, and families in turn influence culture.

Our nation's multicultural origin is rich indeed. Immigrants from every continent have long provided a varied mixture of family styles, configurations, and traditions. Those from England brought a long tradition of nuclear family households, while those from continental, especially southern, Europe, brought more extended family forms. As Europeans interacted with native peoples and moved west, the nature of family life evolved. Independent-pioneer-women-headed households are now being recognized as part of the mix. Intercultural families made up of native peoples and immigrants were more common than is generally acknowledged. The significant presence of African-American families and communities on the western frontier is finally being documented. Thanks to feminist and African-American scholars of the family, a richer picture of the family diversity in the United States is emerging.

This richer picture is powerfully portrayed in the work of Wallace Charles Smith in his book, *The Church in the Life of the Black Family*.[3] Smith has convincingly shown how the sibling-based family structure of West Africa persists among many African Americans who create extended family relationships with people not related biologically or legally. The black church organized itself according to this model of extended family or clan. So, Dr. Smith argues, the situation of a single parent in a black congregation may be very different from the situation of a single parent in a White congregation or in none. A single mother often is supported emotionally and practically by a host of "relatives," and her offspring know the benefit of many male models and a rich climate of acceptance.

Some Recent American Family History

For a moment let's do a thumbnail, necessarily oversimplified, history of families in America. For the last two centuries up to rather recently, two styles of family were dominant in American life. One was the farm family, which tended to be large; more hands made for lighter work. Though some tasks were designated to a single gender, all members were expected to join efforts to achieve the family objective—farming. At harvest time or when disaster struck, families cooperated to get big jobs done. This model was an adaptation of the hunting, migratory family or clan of centuries before. In the 1790 census, the rural population (they did not then distinguish farmers and nonfarmers) was nearly 95 percent of the total. In 1880 nearly 44 percent of all Americans were farmers.

The second dominant family style was the married couple with the husband employed outside the home. These families tended to be smaller because the children were consumers and expensive, rather than part of the labor force. In this family type fewer children benefitted from proportionally more emotional and economic resources. Children were valued for themselves. This was a new era in the history of parent-child relationships. Many children received the kind of attention previously reserved only for royalty.

This family type was probably a first marriage for both father and mother. Increasingly the family lived in suburbia at some distance from the father's work.

Though this family form was considered normative, it was an adaptation, responding to at least two cultural forces. One was the Industrial Revolution, where goods were produced more efficiently than by the individual craftsperson. People no longer worked at home but came to a centralized factory. The other force was public mass transportation and, later, the automobile. These made possible the suburban-dwelling families—living at some distance from the workplace.

Today farm families make up less than 3 percent of the total. Couples (of either first or subsequent marriages) with only the father employed outside the home and with children living at home are somewhere between 7 to 10 percent of all households (about a third of all families with children under eighteen). Folks are concerned about the decrease or demise of this second type of family, but it has its problems also. One observer suggested that the suburban father is often a "boarder with sex privileges." Another wrote: "Each suburban family is somehow a broken home, consisting of a father who appears as an overnight guest [and] a put-upon housewife with too much to do."[4]

Some in the modern men's movement voice a similar anguish. They speak of the removal of children, particularly sons, from their father's influence, guidance, and initiation into manhood. One might describe the scenario in terms of the pressures on fathers and the choices they make to withdraw from participation in their families.

There is much well-placed concern about families. Yet it needs to be viewed in perspective. Such concern is not new. Historian Michael Anderson writes, "Almost no generation has gotten by without debate over family crisis; most problems of our time have also been problems in the past."[5]

Arlene Skolnick cites an exploration of family history that concludes that Americans have been worrying about family life for more than three hundred years.

> Within decades of the Puritans' arrival in Massachusetts Bay Colony, Puritan jeremiads were already decrying the increasing fragility of marriage, the growing selfishness and irresponsibility of parents and the increasing rebelliousness of children.[6]

Times of economic turmoil and recession often stir even greater anxiety about "the family."

Families and Their Present Cultural Milieu

While change for culture and family is a constant, what is new is the frequency, pace, and extent of such change. Here are some of the dominant, fast-breaking developments to which families must adapt:

A Changing Economy and Employment Structure

Some economists suggest that *a vast change is occurring in our economy, a third revolution.* The first was the agricultural revolution, some eight thousand years ago, when humans began to control their environment; they gave up wandering, settled down in one place, planted crops and domesticated animals. The second was the Industrial Revolution, about two hundred years ago, when machines were added to human and animal labor. Production increased by enhancing human energy.

Today we are in the midst of a third revolution, one marked by the development of microelectronics, computers, and robotics. While the Industrial Revolution *enhanced* human energy, in many instances this revolution *replaces* human energy. Through the use of advanced technology, for example, manufacturers have increased their output by more than 400 percent since 1947 with only a 17 percent increase in work-force personnel.[7]

It's not clear what this ultimately will mean as far as employment and livelihood for families. Some contend that this change will be good for employment. Jobs will be available; they will just change in type or nature. Others worry that it will create a permanent underclass of people unable to participate in such an economy.

For the present a wide variety of job opportunities is decreasing—blue collar and more. Computers reduce the need for secretaries. With electronic mail, postal jobs are jeopardized. Automated banking replaces bank tellers. Increased openings seem to be in service jobs, with lower compensation and limited benefits.

For those fortunate enough to have the training and skills, this economic revolution could have marked benefits for family life. For one thing, it could bring the workplace back to the home. In many jobs, if you have a computer, modem, and fax, you can work anywhere.

Declining and Stagnating Economic Opportunity

Change is not the only byword of the economy. For a variety of reasons *many people are experiencing declining or stagnating opportunity.* These disturbing trends have been underway for more than twenty years. Their cumulative effects on millions of families have become impossible to ignore.

Between 1949 and 1973 the average male passing from age twenty-five to thirty-five could expect his real wages would rise by approximately 110 percent. These increases would slow down after age forty, but it was still reasonable to expect a 30 percent increase in earnings from age forty to fifty.

After 1973 twenty-five-year-old males could expect their income to grow by only 16 percent in the next ten years. Those males passing from forty to fifty could expect a decline of 14 percent in those years. The average real wages of women rose modestly over the past two decades, though in many sectors, these wages are seriously below those of men. By 1991 the real weekly earnings of production and nonsupervisory workers, about 80 percent of the work force, had declined to below the level of the early 1960s.[8]

Between 1970 and 1990 the number of workers forced to take part-time positions increased by 121 percent. These workers' wages are about 60 percent of those of full-time workers, and only 22 percent of the part-timers are covered by employer-sponsored health insurance.

Some families have dealt with declining incomes by going deeper into debt. In 1990 an estimated 65 percent of all U.S. households were in debt, either with a mortgage or a consumer loan. About 55 percent of these households owe more than their assets are worth; they have zero or negative financial worth.[9]

Families have been forced to make concessions on what sort of housing they can afford and perhaps to give up the dream of home ownership. In the 1950s two-thirds of all American families could afford the average new house without spending more than 25 percent of their income on mortgage payments. By the 1980s only one in ten could afford the average new dwelling without spending more than a fourth of their income on housing. Some 79 percent of those who could afford to buy a home were two-income couples.

Gaither Lowenstein summarizes:

> The conventional wisdom which has dominated American thinking has been that anyone who works hard, develops skills and applies himself can and will enjoy economic success in the long run. Though this has always been somewhat of a myth, by the beginning of the 1980's the rapid growth of structural unemployment had begun to shatter the dreams of Americans, denying them the promise of upward mobility.[10]

Middle-class families are adjusting by having both husband and wife employed. But their enjoyment of the trappings of economic prosperity may be at the cost of an unharried family life. Even these families may have to make hard choices in terms of affordable colleges for their children.

The economic crunch is impacting the younger generation in terms of postponing marriage, living at home well into adult years, and having fewer children.

The economic crunch has been especially harsh for some families. For example, *young families*—those headed by parents younger than thirty—have seen their real income plummet. The median income for such families dropped by one-third between 1973 and 1990. As a result, 40 percent of children in young families were below the poverty line in 1990, twice the proportion of 1973. *Divorce* has a highly negative economic impact on women and their children. In 1990 the median income for *female-headed households* with children was less than one-third the income for married-couple households with children. When median income figures are analyzed by race and ethnicity, one finds that families of *African-American* and *Hispanic* descent are $13,000 to $15,000 (37 to 42 percent) behind families of Euro-American descent.

Marian Edelman summarizes the pain graphically:

> While the middle class lost ground, the already poor became poorer, more desperate, hungry, homeless, and hopeless. Today, every seventh American is poor as is every sixth family with a child under 18. One out of every five children is poor. If you are a preschooler, the odds are even worse: one out of every four is poor. . . . One out of every two black preschoolers is poor. Two out of every three preschoolers of any background are poor if they live in a female-headed family—and this in the richest nation on earth.[11]

Our economy is destroying families.

Changing Family Demographics

Striking demographic factors, including life expectancy and birth rates, are influencing today's families. In terms of demographics it is difficult to imagine the great gulf between yesterday and today and tomorrow. Peter Uhlenberg notes that the mortality decline in the twentieth century is greater than the total mortality decline in the 250 years preceding it.

Infant and child mortality has dropped. In 1900 fourteen out of every hundred infants died in the first year of life. Today it is fourteen out of every thousand infants. In 1900 half of all parents with three children would see one of them die before age fifteen. Today the probability of parents' losing one out of three children before age fifteen is 6 percent. This in turn has impact on the quality of parent-child relations. As parents were less fearful of losing a child, they grew freer to invest greater emotion and resources in their offspring.[12]

At the same time, the number of children per family has dramatically decreased. At the turn of the century on the average, there were six children per family. It declined to about three children per family in the 1970s. In 1986 the Census Bureau reported an average household size (adults and children living together) of 2.71 people—the lowest since the start of census records. The number of children per family is now about 1.8, less than the population replacement rate of 2.1. Sixty percent of all married couples will have one or two children.[13] It is estimated that 25 percent of women currently of child-bearing age will not have any children at all.

Nevertheless, in the first years of the nineties, the number of births equaled the baby boom years of 1956 and 1963 because the baby boom generation was having babies. Although the number of births to each woman was far fewer than in the fifties and sixties, the sheer number of women having babies increased the number of births.

The interplay of several factors leads to an amazing surprise: The population of the United States is growing. Longer life expectancy, increased immigration, and a higher birth rate than projected are factors in this population growth. The higher birth rate comes from the large cohort of people in the child-bearing years. Following the 1990 census, the Census Bureau boosted its population forecasts. It is now believed that our population will grow by 12 percent in this decade and by 50 percent by the middle of the next century.

This growing population is becoming more ethnically diverse. Currently 74 percent of Americans are descendants of Anglo-European immigrants. This proportion will decrease to 52 percent by 2050. This decrease is affected by immigration and the fact that Euro-American women have a lower fertility rate than African-American and Hispanic women. Americans of Spanish-speaking descent will become the next largest group over the next several decades, growing from some 8 percent of the population to 20 percent. African Americans will increase to 16 percent from their current 12 percent and Americans of Asian descent will grow fivefold to 10 percent of the population. Aboriginal peoples (Native Americans) will reach perhaps 2 percent. The long evolution of American society as a "multicultural salad" will continue and the different ways of being family brought to these shores will continue into the next century. Helping young people appreciate the cultural richness and diversity of American life will be a major task for religious communities over the next several decades.

Yet another demographic fact of life is that the *American population is aging*. At the turn of the century, life expectancy was about fifty. It was nearly seventy in 1955 and had increased to seventy-five by 1990. By the year 2000 the average life expectancy for women will be more than eighty years and may well increase to ninety or more. Russell Chandler points out that half of all Americans who have ever lived past the age of sixty-five are alive now.[14] He also says the fastest growing age segment in the country is those older than eighty-five.

This has led to an increased median age, the age at which half of the population is older and half is younger. Further, the ratio of children under fifteen as a percentage of the population is declining. On the other hand, the proportion of Americans older than sixty-five is growing. In 1991, 54 percent of people over sixty-five lived in married-couple households. Because women live longer than men, about three-quarters of men over sixty-five live with a spouse, but that figure is only 40 percent for women. Most older women, particularly those over seventy-five, live alone. Only 5 percent of all people over sixty-five live in institutions such as nursing homes.

These vast and fast changing demographic factors are having and will have considerable impact on families. Here is a partial list of effects:

1. Families will be freer to love and bond with their children. The smaller number of children may prove to be a good match to the two-paycheck couple or the single parent. Fewer children may be a good match to the parents' decreasing finances; a conservative estimate says it costs $400,000 in 1988 dollars to raise two children through college. Parents' limited time and energy will be directed to one or two children, rather than to several.

2. Children are less likely to be orphaned of one or both parents. They also have a greater chance of knowing grandparents, great-grandparents, and even great-great grandparents. Because the growing number of older people is so recent, it is not clear how four- and five-generation families will relate.

3. Couples who make marriage vows "until death do us part" are making a much longer commitment—from about thirty years at the beginning of this century to at least forty-five years, on the average, today. That means at least another decade and a half of possible life together— all of the joys and frustrations and tragedies that could pull a couple apart. The increase in divorce rates partially reflects the longer life spans of marriages.

4. Parents who have fewer children and live longer will have an extended (twenty-five years or more, on the average) "empty nest" period after children leave home. Previously it was not uncommon for at least one parent to die before the last child left home. The Skolnicks comment, "Actually, the biggest change in twentieth-century marriage is not the proportion of marriages disrupted through divorce, but the potential length of marriage and the number of years spent without children in the home."[15]

5. Child bearing and rearing are no longer a woman's only destiny. Children may or may not be a part of a life plan that includes personal growth, employment, and career. Effective birth control means women have a real choice to have children or not. Those who do have children will have more time both before and after to pursue other interests.

6. The present and future generations of young people will select their intimate partners from an increasingly diverse array of ethnic groups and cultural heritages. More intercultural sensitivities will need to be part of marriage and family skills. Intermarriage, once rare and unusual, is becoming more common. A recent book titled *Mixed Matches: How to Create Successful Interracial, Interethnic, and Interfaith Relationships* speaks to an increasingly widespread phenomenon.[16]

7. Decreased birth rates and growing life expectancy may change the question from "Will the child have grandparents?" to "Will older adults have a grandchild?" A significant minority of older adults may miss out on the experience of grandparenthood.

8. As many more adults survive into their eighties and nineties, they may well need more care from family and others. Some "empty nests"—space vacated by young adult children—may be filled by aging parents who are unable to live independently any longer. It is estimated that 10 percent of people over sixty-five have children who are also over sixty-five! The care given to aged parents may well be stressful and demanding of families. At the same time, the isolation and loneliness of older adults is a family issue that calls for attention and support. The gifts, needs, and issues of older adults in general will need to be a larger agenda item for families and churches.

9. Life expectancy has not been the same for males as for females, and the difference is growing. At the beginning of this century, women could expect to be widows for about four years. Women now can expect to be widows for about ten years.

Changing demographics will have an impact on tomorrow's families.

A Changing Legal Climate

Yet another change is a *strikingly altered legal climate*. In 1970 the State of California instituted the first "no-fault" divorce law, reversing centuries of family law. To comprehend the change, one must be aware of the basis of traditional family law.

Lenore J. Weitzman and Ruth B. Dixon trace the origins of Anglo-American family law to the tenth and eleventh centuries. At that time the medieval church was linked to the state and church teachings on marriage were the law of the land. Legal marriage was firmly grounded in the Christian conception of marriage as a holy union between a man and a woman. Law reflected church convictions that marriage was a sacrament, a commitment to join together for life.

They note five important features of marriage law: (1) Legal marriage was limited to one man and one woman. Bigamy, polygamy, and same-sex unions were prohibited. (2) Legal marriage was monogamous. Sexual fidelity was expected, adultery prohibited. (3) Marriage was for procreation. (4) Legal marriage was hierarchical. The husband was the head of the family, the wife a legal nonperson, "under her husband's arm, protection, and cover." (5) In marriage, family roles and responsibilities were divided by gender, the husband as provider, wife as homemaker and mother.

Marriage was regarded as an indissoluble union that the church and state should protect and preserve. It was hoped that when parties knew they were bound together for life, they would resolve their differences, work out their problems, and make every effort to get along.

While there were variations in divorce law from state to state, in the main the law in the U.S. promoted this point of view. Weitzman and Dixon point to four major elements in traditional divorce laws: (1) sex-based division of roles and responsibilities; (2) required "grounds" for divorce, usually only adultery; sometimes cruelty and/or desertion; (3) adversarial divorce proceedings; (4) financial settlements and child custody arrangements related to the determination of "fault."

With the enactment of the 1970 no-fault legislation in California (and followed in various forms by many other states), the era when law and court enforced traditional church teaching on divorce came to an end. It allowed that the recognition of "marital breakdown" by either or both parties was sufficient basis for divorce. It reversed all four basic elements in traditional divorce law: A new norm of assumed equality between the sexes replaced sex-based role assignments; divorce no longer required assignment of "fault"; the adversarial process was no longer mandated; financial settlement and child custody were based on equity, equality, and need and not on traditional gender roles.[17]

Proponents of this new law had a number of aims. They hoped to eliminate hypocrisy, perjury, and collusion in the courts. There was a desire to reduce acrimony and bitterness in divorce proceedings. Advocates wanted to decrease the stigma that went with divorce. They expected to bring into being the possibility of more rational and equitable settlements of property, spousal support, and provision for children. Such were the lofty hopes.

If some of those goals have been accomplished, there have been at least two unintended negative consequences. For one, no-fault divorce settlements are based on a concept of equality of the sexes; in reality, income possibilities for women are far less than equal. Lenore Weitzman's investigations have revealed that in some cases no-fault divorce hurt women more than the old laws did. One of her studies concluded that in the first year after divorce, women experienced a 73 percent loss in their standard of living, while men's standard of living increased. This loss for women, she said, was irreversible unless the woman remarried. Other studies found that the disparity between women and men, though real, was not as extreme as she asserted. For example, one scholar suggested a 30 percent decrease for women and a 15 percent increase for men was more accurate.[18]

The other unintended consequence has been the astronomical jump in the number of divorces in America—from 393,000 in 1960 to 708,000 in 1970 to nearly 1,200,000 per year in the 1980s and 1990s.

Whether this was the recognition of already failed marriages or encouragement for troubled couples to "quit trying," no one knows for sure. But everyone agrees that with the changed legal climate, divorce is touching nearly every American family. More on this in chapter 2.

Some call for the reform of no-fault divorce laws to make them more just for women and children. Others call for repeal. While changes are possible, clearly the courts will no longer enforce a religious community's concept of marriage. It will be the task of Christian leaders and parents to teach and encourage that understanding themselves.

An Extended and Sometimes Troubled Adolescence

Yet another family change has to do with raising adolescents. In the
1990s adolescence is extending both ways. It is starting sooner. Before
entering the teen years, a youngster may be interested in sex and romance, making decisions about smoking, alcohol, and other drugs, attempting to "grow up." Concerned observers speak of the "hurried child."

If an aspect of adolescence is partial or total dependence on parents,
that season is also extending longer. Many more post-high-school folks
are remaining in their parents' homes while working their first jobs or
attending local commuter colleges. If they go away to school for a while,
they may return home because of job unavailability or low pay. A person
may return to one's family of origin for a time following a divorce.

Among parents of young adults, there used to be a quip that it was
hard to let them go, but even harder to have them return, usually briefly
for summer vacations or winter holidays. Now the return may be longer
lived and require greater adjustments in both generations.

For those in the adolescent years, Fred M. Hechinger notes, there is
great risk:

> large numbers of ten- to fifteen-year-olds suffer from depression
> that may lead to suicide; they jeopardize their future by abusing
> illegal drugs and alcohol, and by smoking; they engage in pre-
> mature, unprotected sexual activity; they are victims or perpetra-
> tors of violence; they lack proper nutrition and exercise.[19]

He points out that by age fifteen, about a quarter of young adolescents
are engaged in behaviors that are harmful or destructive to themselves
or others. An equal number are at moderate risk. Only about half of all
adolescents are growing up basically healthy. Even those, Hechinger
says, lack problem-solving skills.

One of the major impacts on young people is media. Part of the problem, Hechinger points out, is that no one is helping youths learn how to
view and listen to such material critically.

For example, he notes that according to *TV Guide,* American television portrays more than nine thousand acts of suggested intercourse
or innuendo annually, 94 percent involving people not married to each
other. The sexual intercourse portrayed in motion pictures, on video

cassettes, and in rock music largely appears to be carried on without concern for contraceptives, pregnancy, value conflicts, or venereal disease.[20]

This is reflected in adolescent behavior. The average age for first intercourse of American teenagers is 16.2 for girls and 15.7 for boys. Approximately one-third of all fifteen-year-old boys and one-quarter of fifteen-year-old girls have had sexual intercourse.

The birthrates for U.S. White teenagers are higher than those for teenagers in any other Western country and rising. The birthrates for black teenagers is three times as high but falling. Proportionately American girls under eighteen have twice as many babies as British and Canadian girls, more than three times as many as the French, and more than four times as many as the Swedish and the Dutch.

There is another, seldom reported, aspect to teenage pregnancy. It is revealed in such statistics as these: three-quarters of women who had intercourse before age fourteen and almost two-thirds of those who had intercourse before age fifteen report having had sex involuntarily. Further, 19 percent of women between fifteen and nineteen who become mothers are impregnated by men at least six years older than they are. This means that a significant portion of "teenage sexual activity" involves rape, abuse, and coercion of teenaged women by older men. Boyer and Fine interviewed women who became pregnant during adolescence and discovered that two-thirds had suffered rape or sexual abuse at the hands of fathers, stepfathers, other relatives, or guardians.[21]

Any serious response to teen sexuality will have to recognize the role that incest, sexual abuse, and rape plays in it. To reduce the rate of teenage pregnancy will take more than "just say no" campaigns. It requires that we begin socializing boys and men to view women as full persons with the right to say no and make it stick.

In 1988 about 2.5 million adolescents had a sexually transmitted disease. Only 22 percent of sexually active females in that age group said they were currently using condoms, which along with abstinence is the only comparatively safe protection against AIDS. In some ways adolescents are carrying to an extreme the sexual revolution begun some thirty years earlier by their parents.

In 1987 homicide was the third leading cause of death for ten- to nineteen-year-olds. One in sixteen adolescents was a victim of a violent crime. Again, these rates are much higher than for other industrial nations such as Japan, Germany, Australia, and Canada.

Hechinger quotes experts: "Our children are killing each other because we teach violence. We've got to do something to stop the slaughter." Again, these same experts see media as an important influence that must be challenged and changed as regards this message. Children's cartoons routinely portray violence—without pain or ill effect—as an amusing way of life.

> [B]y the time youngsters graduate from high school, many of them will have watched television 22,000 hours, compared to only half that number of hours spent in school. By age eighteen, young people will have been exposed to as many as 18,000 televised murders and 800 suicides.[22]

There is cause for concern about nutrition and diet as well. Again media is a part of the problem. It is estimated that the average young adolescent sees at least ten thousand television commercials advertising food, most of it harmful to one's health. Poor nutrition is part of the problem. Another aspect has to do with girls dieting and susceptibility to eating disorders, as they try to imitate the pencil-thin starlets and models in the public eye. Dieting starts in grade school for nearly a third of all girls. More than half of all high school women have dieted—the majority for appearance rather than health reasons. While fewer males diet, it is estimated that 13 percent of male high school athletes use steroids.

All of these adolescent issues point to yet other preventative, guidance, and care tasks for families as well as to greater stress on families.

A Search for Psychological Satisfactions

There is another change. It is pervasive but more difficult to describe. In recent years there has been a subtle shift in the way folks think and talk about these matters. Americans have become more introspective. They search for self-fulfillment, for growth, for meaningfulness. More people think, talk, and feel in psychological ways about people and processes that matter to them. Arlene Skolnick uses the term "psychological gentrification" to describe this phenomenon. *People recognize, want, and seek psychological and interpersonal fulfillment.*

This in turn leads people to identify what they hope for in marriage and in family life. There is a desire for equality and mutual respect. Husband and wife hope to be best friends, emotional intimates, and great sex partners. Women want men to be involved in child care and transparent about feelings. Men want marriage to be one place where they can be vulnerable and open. There is hope for good ways to resolve conflict. These are high expectations for family life!

All of this is hoped for—with little training in interpersonal skills. People unknowingly hope that other family members will have the human relations skills of highly trained counselors. They come together expecting that family members will "just know how" to respond to the others' needs.

Changes in Gender Roles

Another powerful force affecting families is feminism. The feminist movement that has arisen over the past forty years has touched our most intimate relationships and the whole society in deep ways. Among women it has contributed to new self-understanding, greater awareness and articulation of needs, and an expectation of justice in relationships. The feminist movement has challenged many common, domestic assumptions: that final decision-making power belongs to men; that dominant-submissive relationships are healthy; that violence against wives and sexual abuse of children by male partners and fathers is to be hidden and endured; that the role of women is to serve and accommodate men.

In the public arena, feminism has begun to lay to rest a host of long-standing cultural beliefs: that it is acceptable for our legislatures to be dominated by one gender; that sexual harassment of women by employers is "business as usual"; that women cannot run companies, pastor churches, pilot war planes, or do great science, architecture, or engineering. The struggle to achieve some measure of equality of opportunity for women is still hard fought. In politics, business, law, education, and the church, women find roadblocks at every turn.

Nevertheless, at home or in the public arena, the concept of just social relationships based on fairness and equity is also powerful. The vision of a society in which the gifts of all are valued and used continues to draw forth the commitment of both women and men. Some men are learning how to be allies with women and how to follow their leadership in reinforcing change. The attraction of intimate partnerships in which power is shared and people are free to relate beyond stereotypes and inherited gender roles is too strong to be denied. Here and there, women and men in committed relationships are giving each other permission to identify their real needs and desires.

Families' Response to All This

Families are absorbing these changes, adapting, muddling through. They are attempting to manage with the new economic realities and to adjust to demographic changes. They are trying to be supportive to their children, educating them for a changed future. They do their best to provide guidance and support in struggling with the dangerous realities of growing up. In their rushed schedules, they try to treat each other in ways that fit our new psychological perceptions and needs. New family forms and styles are emerging.

And yet families are not absorbing these changes entirely successfully. There are signs of pain, which we will discuss in chapter 2.

The Church and This Changing Family Scene

Church leaders are not giving a single response to the changing family scene we have been describing. At the risk of oversimplifying, we will describe two tacks being taken by Christian leaders.

One might be described as the biblical traditionalist view. Dr. James Dobson, one of the leading spokesmen, calls people to a traditionalist view that begins with the basic assumption "God is . . . " and gains from Scripture, including the Ten Commandments and the New Testament, a system of thought that touches many dimensions of life.

> Adherents believe (1) in lifelong marriage; (2) in the value of bearing and raising children; (3) in the traditional family, meaning individuals related by marriage, birth or adoption; (4) in the universal

worth of the individual, regardless of productivity or other contributions to mankind; and (5) in a complex series of immutable truths, including premarital chastity, fidelity and loyalty between spouses, the value of self-discipline and hard work, and more.23

Dobson would like to see these values not only practiced by families but promoted and encouraged by the institutions of society. He describes the conflict going on as "a great Civil War of Values," and frequently cites the American Civil Liberties Union and Planned Parenthood as two of his adversaries.

Dobson deeply regrets recent changes in society, recalling that "Until approximately thirty years ago, these biblically based concepts were the dominant values and beliefs in Western society." His perspective is that "never in human history has a culture discarded its belief system more quickly than America did in the sixties."24

He sees current government programs built on the wrong philosophy.

> Social disruption is *inevitable* when government accepts these humanistic tenets: (1) committed, lifelong, faithful families are outmoded or expendable; (2) sexual experimentation of the young is healthy if done "right;" (3) education should be utterly valueless and relativistic; (4) there is no absolute right or wrong . . . no ultimate truth on which to base our decisions; (5) homosexual "preference" is simply another valid lifestyle; (6) he who can work but chooses idleness shall be sheltered and fed; (7) there is no God, and therefore, no transcendent purpose and meaning in living.25

Dr. Dobson's commitment is to a culture, society, church, and to individual families encouraging and practicing the biblical traditionalist principles cited earlier.

There is another way to come at current family issues. Proponents of this other way also apply scriptural insights and Christian convictions to the current family scene.

These folks, however, come to Scripture from a different perspective. They are aware of a wide diversity of family styles within Scripture. They understand that God calls out of history and addresses each family in its cultural context. They see a creative tension between (1) high perfectionist demands regarding human relationships and social justice and (2) radical acceptance and forgiveness for those who fail to meet high standards. These folks discern biblical principles and trends pointing to a liberation of all. They are equally eager to be supportive of strong, healthy families and all that calls such families forth. The authors of this book are in the second group.

Between these two groups there are several areas of likely agreement and also some areas of sharp disagreement. Here are those areas as we see them.

Possible Areas of Agreement

1. Both men and women are created in the image of God.
2. Sex is part of God's creation, a gift for the enjoyment and benefit of humankind.
3. Every effort should be made to help people form and maintain covenanted marriages/partnerships that endure.
4. For personal, family, and societal welfare, it would be good to strengthen marriages and reduce the number of divorces.
5. The welfare and moral guidance of children is of utmost importance to a civilization. All bad treatment, poor example, or wrongful guidance of children deserves to be challenged and held accountable.
6. It is a worthy goal to reduce child and youth sexual involvement and pregnancy and to help young people learn how to form healthy relationships.
7. A worthy goal is less need of abortion services.

Possible Areas of Difference

1. Whether families should be organized in patriarchal or egalitarian patterns.
2. Whether public policies (such as Head Start, food stamps, subsidized housing, and earned income tax credit) strengthen or undermine economically stressed families.
3. Whether abortion services should be permitted by law.

4. Whether a person can ever make an ethically defensible decision to abort.
5. Whether any sex education but abstinence-based education is morally helpful to children and youth.
6. Whether prayer in the schools and voucher-based education strengthen people, families, and society.
7. Whether premarital cohabitation has any moral justification; whether the church can bless a marriage union where people are living together (without their first separating before marriage).
8. Whether no-fault divorce law should be modified or abolished.
9. Whether homosexual orientation can be accepted or should always be treated as a "curable" condition; whether covenanted homosexual union is a defensible moral choice for homosexuals; and whether churches can authentically bless such unions.

We are sure the lists of agreements and differences could both be longer. Each issue we mentioned has a continuum of possible responses. People may find themselves on one "side" on some of the issues of difference and on the other "side" on others. That is quite understandable and even desirable, so long as conversation and dialogue continue to flow. It is tragic when people cut themselves off from fellowship and conversation with those who hold differing views.

The rest of this book deals with a number of the issues on these lists. We shall give much more attention to some than to others, basing our discussion not on the current political debate but on concerns we consider most important for the welfare of families and churches. We believe "returning to traditional family values" is a blind alley, and we are convinced that a new paradigm is emerging for understanding families and for serving them. Ours is another Christian voice on family issues today. We insist that on all of these issues, no one viewpoint "owns" *the* Christian position.

We believe that church leaders are called to be "applied theologians" on family matters. That is, they need to reflect and act on God's revealed will for families within the community and cultural context where they find themselves. To do this, they need: (1) ownership of their basic convictions about human relationships; (2) a grasp of the data—both nationwide and in one's own community; (3) an understanding of family process; and (4) the skills to make helpful input and interventions with families. It is our hope to provide at least beginning help in each of these areas. In the next chapter, we will take a more direct look at families today.

(See our closing epilogue for reflective or discussion questions on each chapter.)

CHAPTER 2

What Are Families Coming to Anyway?
Families in the Nineties and Beyond

*However great the difficulties of the present appear, there is no
point in giving in to the lure of nostalgia. There is no golden age of
family life to long for, no past pattern that, if only we had the moral
will to return to, would guarantee us happiness and security. Family
life is always bound up with the economic, demographic, and
cultural predicaments of specific times and places. We are no longer
a nation of pioneers, Puritans, farmers, or postwar suburbanites.
We must shatter the myths that blind us and find ways to cope with
our present, the place where social change and family history have
brought us.*

—Arlene Skolnick[1]

Meet Ed, a book editor for a publisher in a major city, and his wife,
Doris, a clergywoman. Doris has just finished advanced study and accepted a new job as a pastoral counselor on a preparatory school campus.
They will be moving to a small community almost a thousand miles
away where there are few book editing jobs. Ed is excited about being a
homemaker and a full-time dad of two young boys.

Meet Donna, a single parent in her late twenties. As a teenager in the
throes of rebellion, she had an affair with an older married man of a different race, became pregnant, and bore his child, John. Although her parents stood by her and enjoy their grandson immensely, they do not support her financially. At one time for a few weeks, Donna and John found
themselves literally homeless. The congregation in which Donna grew
up has embraced her and young John and have helped with networking
and emotional support. Currently Donna is working full time and taking
courses toward a nursing degree. Lately she and Bill, a young man who

also grew up in her church, have been seeing each other. Bill has become an important person in John's life.

Meet Hal and Deborah and their two preschool daughters, Elly and Rachel. Hal teaches and Deborah does technical writing for a pharmaceutical company. When Elly was born, Deborah cut down from full-time to part-time to be more involved in parenting. It takes a lot of juggling of schedules for Hal and Deborah to satisfy the expectations of their employers. They can do only so much work at home. Recently the child-care provider they had been using went out of business.

Meet Marge and Sarah and their newborn David. These two professional women decided they wanted to parent. Marge was artificially inseminated with sperm donated by a male friend. They recently joined a congregation open to gay and lesbian people, and there their son was dedicated. They had almost given up hope of finding a "regular" congregation and are thrilled to be in one where David will grow up surrounded by several generations and many fine male role models.

Meet Megan and Ralph and their eleven-year-old daughter Bronwyn. Ruth, Ralph's older daughter from a previous marriage, lives with them during the school year and with her mother during the summer. The transitions in and out of their home are hard for Ruth. She and Megan are often in conflict. Ralph is in school seeking to make a career change. Megan struggles to support the family as a certified social worker with a small private practice.

Meet Amanda and Doug. After several years of temporary jobs, Amanda finally landed a permanent full-time position in a community college where she helps people plan their education. Her husband, Doug, a rising young executive at a major stationery manufacturer, received an attractive offer from another company halfway across the country. They are both deeply committed to each other and to high achievement in their careers. Doug took the job, even though there is some uncertainty about the company's future. So at great cost and personal effort, they maintain contact and lend support to each other—by phone, letter, and at least monthly visits. Perhaps if the new job turns out to be as permanent as it is exciting to Doug, Amanda will look for a job in the new city. Until then, theirs is a commuter marriage.

Meet Grace and Tom, in their early fifties. Their oldest child is launched; a second is finishing college, and one is still at home. Recently Grace has been appointed guardian of her ninety-year-old mother and eighty-seven-year-old father. She moved them from their home in another state into an assisted-living community about forty-five minutes away from her house. Their adjustment to the new living arrangement is bumpy, and she is frequently asked by the facility manager to help gain her parents' cooperation.

These are true stories of real people. All of them are involved in congregations. You will meet families with similar issues in most congregations, including yours. The variety of their situations and needs leads us to think about family ministry in some new ways. In this chapter we present a picture of what is happening to families in the nineties and what are some likely developments in family life as we move into the next century. Keep these vignettes in mind. They make sense of the statistical information that follows.

A Definition

In chapter 1 we noted the historical diversity of family life on the North American continent. We reviewed the impact of industrialization and accompanying development of the suburbs on family structure and style. We then focused on the economic and social forces driving massive changes in the form and function of all families over the last two decades. The extent and rapid pace of the changes we are witnessing have unsettled many thoughtful people. Even the idea of *family* has become both confused and controversial. Those of us who believe that families play an irreplaceable role in the development of the next generation had better be sure we are clear what we mean by *family*.

The sheer variety of configurations claiming to be family throw doubt on the notion that everyone knows what a family is. Arguments rage among scholars and talk-show hosts about what a family is or must be. Simply describing kinds of families is difficult because applicable terms are often differently defined by demographers, Census Bureau reports, and journalists. Each uses a different framework to depict family and household realities. In this chapter we will describe the diversity of familial relationships and households present and emerging in American society today. First, however, we will attempt to say clearly what *we* mean by the term *family*.

We understand the concept of family to mean any network of two or more people linked over time emotionally and usually biologically and legally, sharing such things as home, spiritual and material resources, interpersonal care giving, memory, common agenda, and aspirations.

We recognize the need to defend this definition. It is based in systems thinking. The concept of family as an emotional, social, and often biological system in which every member is affected by and affects every other is an important part of the new paradigm for understanding families set forth in this book. If you want convincing evidence for the reality of family systems, watch a family interact on video tape with the sound turned off; simply concentrate on the choreography. Every member present provokes and responds to every other in observable, physical patterns that become predictable if you watch long enough. Family systems have the kind of tangible reality that can be seen, measured, recorded, and analyzed.

To get a sense of the reality of a family system, try this thought exercise. Imagine the family in which you grew up doing some activity together, perhaps playing a game, eating, traveling, fighting, or working outside. Picture the physical relationships, the facial expressions, the gestures. Who is giving leadership? Who participates? Who is excluded or put down? Who brings the whole family to a halt by some comment or behavior? What predictable, repetitive patterns do you observe? What, then, does your family's pattern of interaction say about how power, gender, competence, and emotional connection operate in the group that was your family of origin? Can you sense the physical, spiritual, and emotional power of that group in your life then and now?

Our definition of family is more empirical than ideological. It takes *what is* seriously before affirming *what should be*. It rests on the assumption that emotional linkages are at least as powerful as biological and legal ones. It does not assume "living under one roof" as a necessary criterion; family ties are known to bind people who live a continent apart. In this respect, our definition differs from that of the Census Bureau, which reserves the label *family* only for two or more people related by blood, marriage, or adoption and who share a kitchen. Our definition does not exclude such units, but it assumes that emotional ties are more important than sharing a kitchen.

Our definition does not regard procreation or even the potential to be procreative as central to the "familyness" of a couple. This definition can include a straight, gay, or lesbian couple in a long-lived committed relationship or a group of unmarried people who commit to living communally. What counts in our view are the visible interactions of a family system. Where those emotional and physical connections are present, family is present. Legal and biological linkages, though very important, are nevertheless secondary to the emotional and behavioral.

By saying a family is two or more people, we do not exclude single adults living alone. We simply see a family as a system, and a system is by definition divisible into its parts and their relations. We've yet to meet a single person who came into this world outside a family system or lives unaffected by that or another family system. Even to be cut off from one's family is to be affected by one's family. Many single people of our acquaintance have cultivated intimate family relationships with other single people, with nuclear family units to which they are not legally or biologically related, and of course with their own kin. They may play important member roles in several family systems.

We believe that our definition fits the reality of contemporary family experience even as it includes the diversity of household and kinship patterns that have historically characterized life on this continent. Our definition also respects the varied family and kinship traditions of those who have migrated to America from the other continents. This definition can address the complexity of the biblical patriarch's kinship system as well as the familial quality of life among Jesus and his disciples portrayed in the Gospels.

We further believe that today's families, as diverse as they are, can be touched by the ministry of the church and helped to become more satisfying, joyful, and life-affirming. Chapters 4 and 5 will focus on the ways such ministry can take place. To make this point, however, we need to review the data relevant to family life in the 1990s as well as look ahead realistically to see where the trends of the data are taking us.

While looking at the trends, remember that the common tendency to take the 1950s as a baseline is to make an exceptional decade the norm. In actuality, for example, the divorce rate has been rising for a century. Some measures, such as the median age at first marriage, have returned to where they were at the end of the nineteenth century. It is useful to put the rapid changes in family life of the late sixties and seventies in a long-term perspective.

Marriage, Divorce, and Remarriage

Marriage, divorce, and remarriage rates are key to understanding the diversity of family configurations in contemporary America. They give us a picture of millions of personal decisions that result in the formation, disruption, and rearrangement of families characteristic of our time. The graph below shows rates of first marriage, divorce, and remarriage rates from 1921 to 1989.[2] The most interesting thing to note is the relative stability of rates since 1980. The rapid changes we saw in the sixties are unlikely in the nineties because the population is aging.

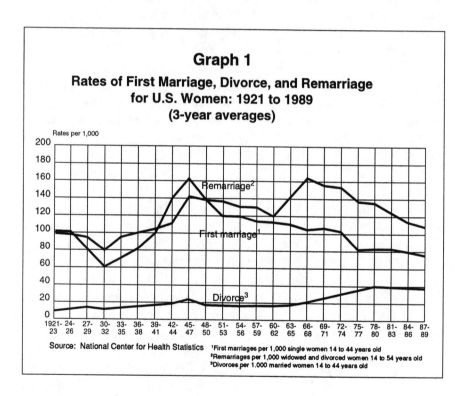

Graph 1

**Rates of First Marriage, Divorce, and Remarriage
for U.S. Women: 1921 to 1989
(3-year averages)**

Source: National Center for Health Statistics   [1]First marriages per 1,000 single women 14 to 44 years old
[2]Remarriages per 1,000 widowed and divorced women 14 to 54 years old
[3]Divorces per 1,000 married women 14 to 44 years old

Marriage Rates

The following graph shows two marriage rates. One can look at the number of marriages per one thousand population, which has been fairly steady over the last several years, or one can measure the number of marriages per one thousand unmarried women ages fifteen to forty-four, which has declined dramatically since the mid-1970s.[3] The first rate gives a more general picture of marriage formation while the latter focuses on the segment of the population most eligible for a first marriage.

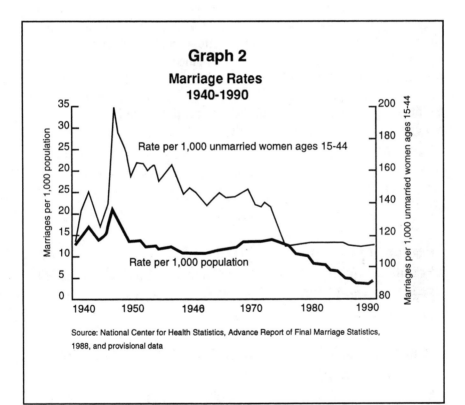

Graph 2
Marriage Rates
1940-1990

Source: National Center for Health Statistics, Advance Report of Final Marriage Statistics, 1988, and provisional data

The marriage rate per one thousand population has remained steady and yet the number of marriages has reached an all-time high. Why? Because the large baby boom generation reached marriageable age in the 1980s. The rate of marriage for eligible women dropped because the baby boomers have been marrying at later and later ages. This shows up in the statistic for median age at first marriage.

The median age for first marriage has been moving up steadily since the late 1950s. It now stands at twenty-six years for men (exactly where the figure stood in 1890!), up from 22.6 in 1955. For women, the median age of first marriage is the highest it has ever been since measurements have been kept: almost twenty-four, up nearly four years from its 1955 low, and up almost two years from the 1890 figure.

At the same time, the percent of population that has never married is growing. This is shown in the table below. The growth of the young adult never-married population is dramatic, especially when measured against the numbers for 1960. For women, the proportion of never marrieds in the youngest age group more than doubled, and it nearly tripled in the two older age groups. For the men in the youngest group, the number of never marrieds has increased 50 percent over the thirty years and more than doubled for the older age groups.[4]

Table 1

Percent unmarried	1960	1980	1990
Females age 20-24	28.4%	50.2%	62.8%
Females age 25-29	10.5%	20.9%	31.1%
Females age 30-34	6.9%	9.5%	16.4%
Males age 20-24	53.1%	68.8%	79.3%
Males age 25-29	20.8%	31.1%	45.0%
Males age 30-34	11.9%	15.9%	27.0%

The racial differences in marriage patterns have also changed. Before World War II, similar proportions of Blacks and Whites married, with Blacks tending to marry at a younger age. Today the average age of marriage for Blacks is two years older than that for Whites, and a smaller proportion of black women marry. While in 1990, 95 percent of women and men aged forty-five to fifty-four had been married at least once, a recent study projects that about 12 percent of white women and one-fourth of black women aged thirty to thirty-four in 1990 will never marry.[5]

We see three reasons for the changing marriage patterns. Cohabitation appears to be the most significant factor. Between 1970 and 1990 the percentage of couples cohabiting prior to a first marriage increased from 11 percent to nearly 50 percent. Forty percent of cohabiting couples have children living with them, from previous marriages or their own union. One-fourth of unmarried births are to cohabiting couples.

Some researchers argue that the declining marriage rate is largely offset by increases in cohabitation. Basing their conclusions on the National Survey of Families and Households (a survey conducted in 1987-88 of more than thirteen thousand people), Larry Bumpass and his colleagues found that young people are setting up housekeeping with a partner of the opposite sex at almost as early an age as they did before marriage rates declined. Three-fourths of the decline in the proportion of twenty-five-year-old women married for the first time is offset by increased cohabitation. All of the decline in the proportion of separated and divorced people who remarried within five years of divorce or separation was offset by increased cohabitation.[6]

By analyzing this survey of a representative sample of the U.S. population, Bumpass and associates made several interesting discoveries:

- Cohabitation compensates for the drop in marriage rates more among females than males, more among Blacks than Whites, and more among the less educated than the well educated. The more economically and socially marginalized the group, the more cohabitation is replacing marriage. (This interpretation of the data is consistent with what church leaders report about cohabitation around the world.[7])

- Cohabitation is not a pattern that began among "radical" college students and spread to the rest of the population of young adults.

Rather, cohabitation has long been a pattern among the least educated and most economically deprived. Beginning in the 1960s it
spread up the social class scale.

- Cohabitation is growing today only among the less educated and
  among divorced and separated people where it is more common than
  among the never married.

- Cohabitation is actually declining among college-educated young
  people, though it is still wide-spread.

The decline of marriage rates is often linked to a second factor: new
career options for women. As women's education and employment opportunities improved, so did their earning capacity relative to men's. The
economic incentive for women to marry lessened. At the same time, the
earnings of young men began to stagnate, making marriage less affordable for them. Men's earnings rose in the 1950s but then declined 20
percent between 1972 and 1989. The decline was even more significant
for minority men. William Julius Wilson has documented the relationship between loss of high-paying manufacturing jobs and the steep decline in marriage rates among African Americans.[8]

A third explanation for declining marriage rates over the last several
decades is the "marriage squeeze." Women tend to marry older men and
the supply of "older men" rises and falls with the changes in the birth
rates. Women who were born in the early 1950s (the first half of the baby boom) were faced with far fewer older men to marry and so rates
dropped in the early 1970s.

As we have seen, even the dramatic increase in cohabitation is related to economic forces as well as to changing evaluations of marriage
as a personal choice.

Divorce Rates

Figure 1 gave a picture of divorce over the middle six decades of this
century. The rate has increased throughout that time with a peak immedi-
ately following World War II and then a steady rise beginning in the
midsixties. The rate has leveled off and declined slightly as married baby

boomers move through the years when divorce is most likely. The divorce rate in the U.S. is the highest in the industrialized world and stabilized in the 1980s at a historically high level.

How shall we view these facts? Perhaps a historical perspective will help. To begin with, divorce has been generally illegal in Europe until recent times, while it has always been legal in the United States. Since the first recorded colonial divorce in 1649, the upward trend of the divorce rate has been virtually unbroken. Further, the combination of premature death of a spouse, divorce, and desertion in the last half of the nineteenth century contributed to a rate of family disruption only somewhat less than what is experienced today. Keep in mind that the divorce rate includes not only disrupted first marriages, but also second and later marriages, which have a higher divorce rate than first marriages. Finally, the increase in U.S. divorce rates in recent decades is matched by only slightly lower increases in divorce rates throughout the industrialized world. This fact suggests that worldwide social and economic forces are at work making marriages less likely to endure.

Remarriage

Most Americans who divorce also remarry. In 1988 one-third of all marriages were remarriages for at least one of the partners and about one-fifth of existing marriages include at least one previously divorced person.[9] The high rate of remarriage is driven by the high rate of divorce; that is, there are many former partners "eligible" for remarriage. The time between marriages has been increasing, paralleling the delay of first marriages, as noted above.

There are important gender and racial differences in remarriage. Men remarry sooner and in a greater proportion than women. Five out of six divorced men remarry compared to three out of four women. African-American women are less likely and slower to remarry than divorced white women. Women over forty have a low probability of remarriage, although the remarriage rate for older widows is increasing. For African Americans, remarriages are more enduring than first marriages (the opposite for white couples), although divorce rates are higher for both first marriages and remarriages among African Americans.

Some Reflections

When the Census Bureau estimates that half of all marriages occurring since 1970 will end in divorce, it is a cause of concern for pastors. We are involved in weddings and must wonder why so many of the marriages we know best end in divorce. Is divorce a sign of deteriorating values in our society? Several causes for the high divorce rate seem worth considering.

First, it may be that this generation of Americans values *successful* marriage more highly than did their parents and grandparents. As we noted earlier, expectations for marriage have risen and tolerance for an unsatisfying union has dropped. Divorce seems more acceptable than continued unhappiness. The high rate of remarriage is evidence for this interpretation. The remarriage rate suggests that there is not widespread disillusionment with marriage. Rather, divorce is driven by dissatisfaction with a particular spouse. The tendency to "try, try again" is powerful!

Certainly the no-fault divorce law revolution has made divorce easier. Without the requirement of proving that one party has failed to keep the contract, the stigma of divorce is lessened. At the same time, the way is now open for one partner to terminate the marriage even without the consent of the other. What in an earlier time might have been a desertion is now a divorce. Custody of children and division of property have become the major issues confronting divorcing couples.

Economic changes have had a part in changing patterns of divorce. Women's massive entry into the work force has challenged the traditional division of labor within the family and freed women from economic dependence on a husband. These changes in turn have reduced the amount of domestic support and deference in decision making that men enjoyed a generation ago. Greater economic independence means women no longer need to remain in an abusive or emotionally unsatisfying relationship.

Popular attitudes have changed toward divorce. While most express belief in marriage as a lifetime commitment, the share of Americans who believe a couple should stay together in an unhappy marriage for the sake of the children has diminished markedly. In 1962 a survey of young mothers found that half of them believed a couple should stay together for the sake of the children. But when the same women were asked the same question in 1985, the proportion who still believed a couple should stay together for the welfare of the children fell to less than 20 percent. The shift in attitude was even more dramatic when polling the young adult offspring of these women. Ninety percent of the daughters and 70 percent of the sons stated that unhappy couples, even with children, should not stay together.[10]

It seems clear that few any longer view marriage as an institution to be preserved at all cost. Instead, marriage has come to be seen as a relationship that is expected to be emotionally gratifying for the partners. When it fails to be so, many make the choice of ending the relationship and trying again with another partner, either in marriage or in cohabitation.

Some are now speaking with alarm of a "culture of divorce" that has displaced the "marriage culture" in America. These voices are calling for a "fundamental shift in cultural values and public policy" toward strengthening marriage.[11] In their publication *Marriage in America: A Report to the Nation,* scholars and critics related to The Council on Families in America (sponsored by the Institute for American Values) express their concern about the welfare of children and the negative consequences of growing up without a stable family. Their report focuses only in passing on the nature of marriage relationships and instead highlights the function of marriage in society. So while they criticize the individualism that drives partners out of unsatisfying relationships, they fail to consider the expectations partners bring to a marriage. As we have pointed out, couples have the prospect of many years together, only a relatively small portion given to child bearing. Exhortations to value marriage for the sake of the children are unlikely to be all that persuasive.

Neither is a similar Christian response to marriage and divorce patterns that seeks merely to "reinstitutionalize" marriage likely to succeed. A response more deeply rooted in Christian spirituality and commitment is required.

As we have rethought the meaning of marriage for Christians and practical ways to minister, we suggest considering marriage from the perspective of vocation. A basic Christian understanding is that we are called by the Holy Spirit into committed relationships. Committing to a partner is a decision of discipleship, and the rationale for such a commitment is not only what it promises in emotional fulfillment, but also what it offers the two partners in terms of growth in faith, witness, and love.

Such a perspective makes sense only when applied to a marriage between fellow believers and distinguishes Christian marriage from purely secular relationships. It does suggest that clergy counseling with couples ought to probe the faith commitments of the prospective partners and how they see their partnership enriching their individual lives as disciples.

Pastors and other church leaders may not be able to reverse the high divorce rate. But they may be able to impact Christian marriages positively by the quality of premarital counseling they offer and by giving attention to the development of enrichment opportunities for the couples in their care.

Major Changes in Households

The changes in rates of marriage, divorce, remarriage, and unmarried cohabitation discussed above and the child-bearing patterns described in chapter 1 make for the diversity of family configurations in the U.S. today. This proliferation of household types as measured by the U.S. Census leads to a complex meaning of *family*. Let's look more closely at the ways contemporary families are put together.

More Nonfamily Households

The percentage of "non-family households" (as defined by the Census Bureau) has doubled between 1960 and 1991.

Remember the Census Bureau definition of *family* as two or more people related by blood, marriage, or adoption and sharing a dwelling; all others are "non-family households." A nonfamily household is one in which a person lives alone or with unrelated others. These households include a diverse range of people, including anyone living alone; college-aged youth sharing an apartment; cohabiting couples; and people "between marriages." The increase in nonfamily households is depicted in the pie charts below.[12]

Fewer Households with Two Parents and Children

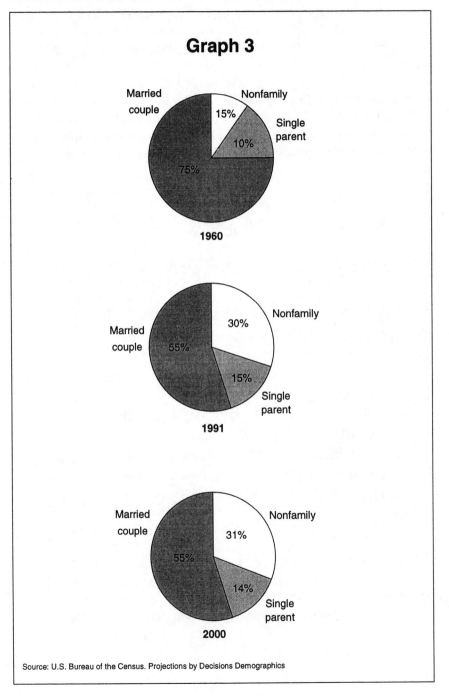

Graph 3

1960

1991

2000

Source: U.S. Bureau of the Census. Projections by Decisions Demographics

Keep in mind that these charts do not "prove" that family ties are weakening since they show only living arrangements, not emotional connections. They do illustrate the impact of trends such as longer life spans (older people living alone) and the increase in age of first marriages.

The percentage of families comprising two parents and their children under eighteen (the popular image of "family") has declined from half of all families in 1970 to 36 percent of families in 1991.

The proportion of such families is projected to decline further to a little over one-third by the year 2000. The table below illustrates these changes.13

Table 2

Family Composition in the United States, 1970-2000

Type of Family	1970	1990	1995	2000
All families (in millions)	51.2	64.5	68.09	71.7
Total	100.0%	100.0%	100.0%	100.0%
Married couple with children	49.6	36.9	36.2	34.5
Married couple without children	37.1	41.7	41.8	42.8
Female head with children	5.7	10.2	10.0	9.7
Male head with children	0.7	1.8	2.2	2.7
Other families	6.9	9.4	9.8	10.3

Source: Projections prepared by Decision Demographics. Data for 1970 from U.S. Bureau of the Census, *Current Population Reports* P-20, no. 218.

Over the last two decades there has been significant growth in the "married couple without children" (under eighteen living at home) category. Longer life spans, the aging of the population as a whole, and later age of marriage are significant reasons for this increase in the percentage of couples without children. One would expect that this category will continue to grow as a proportion of households.

More Single-Parent Households

The percentage of single-parent families has almost doubled from 1970 to 1990.

One in five Euro-American families with children is a single-parent family, as is one in three Hispanic families with children and six in ten African-American families with children. Larry Bumpass believes

About half of today's young children will spend some time in a single-parent family, most as a consequence of divorce. . . . Further more, this is not just simply a transitional phase between a first and second marriage. The majority will reside in a mother-only family for the remainder of their childhood.[14]

This change has provoked the most concern among observers because the outcomes for children in single-parent homes are consistently found to be poorer than for children in two-parent homes. A high divorce rate and a dramatic increase in out-of-wedlock childbearing account for this change. In chapter 5 we will explore ways to strengthen such families.

Signs of Families under Stress

Much of the demographic data we have reviewed above describes conditions contributing to a variety of negative outcomes for children and families. Many studies indicate that the rate of "at risk behaviors" is higher for youngsters in single-parent rather than two-parent households. The percentage of children in poverty is growing. Child abuse, wife battering, incest, adolescent suicide, date rape, as well as personal attacks on those perceived to be homosexual, and the killing of young people in their schools and on the streets add up to an unprecedented level of family and community violence. Levels of alcohol and drug addiction are climbing among young people and adults, with increasing numbers of babies born already addicted and/or with AIDS. All this adds up to *stressed families*. Let's take a closer look at these stresses on families and the resulting negative outcomes, especially for children.

Economic Stress

As indicated in chapter 1, downward economic mobility, a reality for many families, is impacting family well-being. In a now classic 1980s study of working-class black families, Lewis and Looney found that below a minimum threshold of income, no families in the sample were functioning in a healthy manner. Above the threshold, the researchers saw the whole range of family functioning.[15]

Low family income and the lack of health insurance produces grave consequences for the physical health of families. An estimated one-fourth of pregnant women receive no prenatal care. Thirty percent of American children receive inadequate medical care. Twenty percent do not see a physician over the course of a year. Half of American children under fifteen have never visited a dentist. Two of every five preschoolers have not received immunizations.[16]

At the absolute bottom of the economic ladder are homeless families. A 1987 survey of homeless people found that one-fourth are in family units: 15 percent are children; 8 percent are parents (almost always single mothers); and 2 percent are married couples without children. This means on a given night, between 125,000 and 150,000 families are homeless. These numbers reflect only a snapshot view of the problem. The number of families that experience homelessness over a year's time is much greater. The average homeless episode for a mother and her children is sixteen months. Few of these families receive income from government programs. One-third of the mothers in the study received AFDC, another third general assistance, and only about half received food stamps. One sixth of the mothers were employed.[17]

Church strategies to strengthen families, if they are to go beyond soothing symptoms, must include efforts to influence economic policies, for example the minimum wage. When first instituted, minimum wages

were sufficient to keep families above the poverty line. For that to be true
in the midnineties, minimum wages would have to be more than six
dollars an hour. Economic justice for families is essential to improving
the longevity of marriages and the quality of parenting.

The Pain of Abuse

The most dangerous place for a woman to be is in her own home. Violence occurs at least once in two-thirds of all marriages. And one in four
marriages suffers ongoing violence. A woman's most likely assailant is
her male partner. Over half the men who batter their partners batter the
children in the household as well. There are 1.7 million reported cases of
child abuse and neglect annually and two thousand deaths of children
each year resulting from abuse. Such abuse contributes to a cycle of
violence: abused children are 53 percent more likely to be arrested as
juveniles and 38 percent more likely to be arrested as adults for criminal
activity. There are no statistics measuring the extent of verbal, emotional,
and spiritual abuse in families. But the numbers of adults participating in
self-help groups and twelve-step programs for survivors of dysfunctional
families suggest this is a tragic reality in many homes.[18]

Family Resilience

In the face of such stress, families show remarkable resilience. To maintain income in middle-class households, families have put more of their
members to work. In two-parent households, three-quarters of mothers
with school-aged children work for pay outside the home.[19] In addition,
over 80 percent of single parents work outside the home, contradicting
the stereotype of the welfare-dependent single mother.

Child care is an enormous issue for these families. Among a rapidly
growing number of two-parent families, fathers are taking on this responsibility. Two million fathers have decided to be their children's primary
caregivers. Twenty percent of preschool children are cared for by their
fathers while their mothers work, almost matching the percentage of
children in organized day-care programs. These stay-at-home dads are
organizing, too, with a quarterly newsletter published by a stay-at-home

dad.[20] Many of these fathers have been displaced by corporate down-sizing. Rather than accepting a low-paying job and paying child-care costs, they have chosen to do the child care while their wives take advantage of expanded work opportunities for women.

A significant portion of these at-home dads are starting businesses they can do from their home. In fact, self-employment doubled between 1970 and 1990 and is rising faster than at any time in this century. One estimate is that by 2000 one-fifth of us will earn our principal income through self-employment.[21]

Working from home is on the rise among salaried employees as well. Responding to the desires of working parents and to environmental concerns, some employers are adopting flex-place strategies. This also increases the available labor pool, giving employers access to millions of unemployed and underemployed workers with disabilities. By the end of the decade, an estimated 10 to 15 percent of salaried work will be done in the home.

The extended family has made a significant comeback. In 1980 slightly over half of all eighteen- to twenty-four-year-olds lived with parents. Today two-thirds live with parents. At the same time, the high cost of care for the very aged is leading more and more families to take on this task. Surveys of employees indicate that a quarter of all workers are caring for an elderly relative near or in their homes. Families have spent hundreds of billions remodeling their homes to accommodate both home-grown businesses and dependent family members.[22]

Such changes as these do not often make headlines, but they are evidence of major social transformation. They speak of family strength and resilience in spite of tremendous economic challenges. They demonstrate the power of family systems to adapt to new realities. They remind us that families create as well as adapt to culture. Family agenda, when carried into the public sphere, can fuel social change.

For example, consider the commitment of countless married couples over the last two decades that has created a substantial lay-led marriage enrichment movement. Or the work of the interfaith Parenting for Peace and Justice Network.[23] It links thousands of families in this country and overseas to one another and to a set of values for living in families and in global community. Or consider the groundswell of African-American churchmen creating mentoring programs for fatherless young boys.[24] These determined men model competence and compassion to youngsters often living in massively impoverished neighborhoods where drugs are as available as candy, the schools are bankrupt, single parents are over-whelmed, and despair abounds.

Such initiatives created by resilient families call for sensitive and imaginative responses from congregations. Ministries *to* families are needed, but so are *partnerships with* families advocating for public poli-cies that take into account the important work families do on behalf of the entire society. The remarkable resilience of families should not be taken for granted but should be seen as a gift of God's grace to the hu-man community. Given the declining economic prospects over the next decade for millions of us, thoughtful family advocates are challenged to craft public policy initiatives that support families in their care-giving functions and reward them for economic innovation. Our society cannot fiscally afford to replace the work families do.

A New Paradigm

The new day for family ministries requires a new paradigm. Now, after defining *family* and describing contemporary family *realities,* we are ready to point out some of the key elements in this new paradigm.

- We should not speak about "the family" but about "families" and include in our understanding more types of relationships than ever before.

- Contemporary families have a variety of members, styles, and deci-sion-making processes.

- Relationships in contemporary families vary in duration; such in-stability does not invalidate their importance. Indeed some family configurations such as half-way houses and foster families are suc-cessful *if* they can help people to move on.

- Contemporary families have fewer institutional norms and predict-able patterns to guide them. They have to work out their relation-ships through deliberate negotiation and planning.

- Contemporary families have great needs for teaching, guidance, and counsel about how to live out their calling as families.

- Families today need pastors and church leaders who have fewer presumptions about them and more willingness to listen to their unique needs.

- Church leaders who want to help families endure in today's culture are called to an educational task: to teach families how to negotiate needs and meet one another's needs in a spirit of mutuality. They must teach families how to enter, keep, and rebuild committed relationships.

One further reflection about ministering with the diverse family configurations we've described in this chapter: As pastors and church educators, we are dealing with specific families in specific social, economic, and spiritual circumstances. While an awareness of social trends can put a particular family's agonies and triumphs in perspective, one cannot generalize from statistical information what is spiritually healthy for that unique family whose care is our responsibility. The facts of social change can give us information about what we may face in our ministries. They can help us identify challenges and opportunities. But interpreting social trends and developing faithful ministries that engage the families in our care remains our creative responsibility.

In the next three chapters, we will search for theological and ethical insights and practical strategies that will lead us to a new paradigm for family ministries that is adequate to our new understanding of who families are today.

CHAPTER 3

A Christian Theological-Ethical Response

We are so captive to an image of the Christian family that we cannot minister to the pain of contemporary family life. Most often the church does not see how it really is in our families or, if it does, it looks the other way until all appears well again. . . .

The tensions of family life are never ending. Through the Holy Family, God has experienced them all. In our families there are unexpected teenage pregnancies, shaky marriages, questions of divorce, parent-child conflicts, single parent families, sickness and weakness, aging parents and death. There is great hope and encouragement that in the Holy Family, God has experienced all of these. God's earthly family was like mine—broken and yet whole, loving, and liberating. May our broken families be for us holy—giving us wholeness, love, and liberty.

—Willie S. Teague[1]

Up to this point, we have been reporting critical facts about families in America. How did they get to their current state? What are the current cultural impacts on them? How diverse are families? What are signs of health, pain, and resiliency among them?

Now our task changes from description to prescription. What ethical mandates would we offer families and churches? What is the church called to be and do in the face of the changing family scene? We move on to navigate these waters with you.

In this chapter we will set forth our Christian ethical assumptions and method. We will also explore a number of aspects of a biblical-theological perspective. In chapters 4 and 5 we will apply this perspective to the issues facing families today.

On Theological Ethical Method

Sources of Guidance

As we seek to know God's will for church leaders ministering with contemporary families, we propose a round-table dialogue of four equal partners: (1) Scripture; (2) personal experience; (3) the wisdom of the church, past and present; and (4) discoveries and insight from social science research. This information helps us identify the present situation and effective and ineffective means of dealing with issues and problems.

Our dialogue among these four partners needs to be humble. The tendency to self-deception is enormous. Unbiased research is rare, if possible. So we offer a defensible position and submit it to vigorous critique by our believing colleagues. In this way we move toward clarity about the divine will for churches and families today and tomorrow.

Faithfulness within One's Culture

We face another challenge—to determine our stance as people of faith toward our culture. How are we faithful to a conviction when the odds are stacked against us?

Decades ago H. Richard Niebuhr created a clarifying typology for this. On the extremes were "Christ against culture" (where Christ is seen as opposing many of culture's norms) and "Christ of culture" (in which the current culture is affirmed and accepted). A continuum ranged from views that attempted to escape culture . . . to live with paradoxical demands of both Christ and culture . . . or to transform culture.[2] We favor the last alternative.

We live in a culture that does not honor Christian values. By that we don't bemoan only the litany of sins identified by our colleagues on the right—increases in premarital sexual behavior, divorce, nonmarital cohabitation, and out-of-wedlock pregnancy. These are surely problematic for Christians, and we will examine these concerns. There are other issues as well. Our society is violent. It is barely outraged by the sexual abuse of children and the beating of wives. It is indifferent to a quarter of our children living in poverty and has seemingly no will to address the obscenity of families living on the street. As we write, the Congress is systematically shredding the social safety net for families and children that took decades to construct. Both the Congress and many state houses have sent a clear message to the most impoverished and vulnerable members of our society: *You are so much excess baggage. Would you please go away?*

In the face of this challenge, we see three choices facing Christian leaders: (a) Relate to people and families in their present circumstances. (b) Join efforts to move the culture closer to scriptural ideals for both personal and social relationships. And (c) create a Christian counter culture with those who are committed to right relationships among people and justice in the society.

We believe the Christian leader needs to be committed to all three options and in this priority: (a), (c), (b).

Biblical Revelation and Families

In good company, we view the Bible as the book of the acts of God. The Bible reveals God entering into history, acting to redeem a people, entering into covenant with them. This covenant with a particular people is so that all the people of the earth may be blessed. In the fullness of time, God renewed the covenant through the life, death, and resurrection of Jesus of Nazareth. Jesus' followers were commissioned and empowered to carry this saving story to the ends of the earth.

The Bible tells not only the story of our salvation, but it also offers us guidance and instruction, worship materials, wisdom sayings, erotic poetry, and more.

We must note that in the Bible, "family" as we think of it is not a central topic. Families were among many players in the drama—including individual people, clans, nations, and empires—responding to the revealed will of God. But some families were significant players and their stories are illuminating.

The Bible story is played out in a wide array of geographical settings, cultures, and times. It covers hundreds upon hundreds of years. Biblical portrayals of family life and teaching about family responsibilities reflect this changing milieu. We see a trajectory running through biblical teachings about family relationships, reaching profound revolutionary insight—particularly for its cultural setting—in Ephesians 5-6.

Having said all this, we identify a number of basic biblical teachings about intimate partnerships and family life.

Covenantal Relationships

Covenantal relationships are basic to right relationship among people and with God. Living in covenant with others and with God is a fundamental theme in both testaments. Consider God's covenants with Noah, the patriarchs, David, and the people of Israel. In terms of human relationships, covenant is critical to the relationship of Abraham and Lot, the petition of Hannah for parenthood, the friendship of Jonathan and David, the marriage of Hosea and Gomer, the joint venture of Ruth and Naomi. Marriage is seen as a covenantal relationship, initially between families and finally between husband and wife. So it is not surprising that one biblical statement about marriage is quoted more than any other—both within the Bible and without. It comes from Genesis 2, the creation accounts. God brings the woman whom God has created to the man and Adam ex-claims, "This at last is bone of my bones / and flesh of my flesh," and the passage concludes, "Therefore a man leaves his father and his mother and clings to his wife, and they become one flesh" (Gen. 2:23-24).

The union of man and woman is created by God. It is intended to be "one flesh"—a deep interpersonal and sexual union. It is meant to be a partnership based on faithfulness, trust, and truth telling. It is meant to be unbroken. Different cultures and ages will have varying ways to live out this truth. The divine intent, however, is enduring.

People often fall short of God's intention. They did so then and do so now. Still, people are called to be as faithful to the covenants they make as God is to the covenant God has made with us. Human faithfulness is a reminder and reflection of the faithfulness of God.

Biblical Variety

Within the Bible, there is a tremendous variety of family forms and styles. Sometimes these exemplify covenant relationships; sometimes they do not.

Virginia Ramey Mollenkott has cataloged forty diverse forms of family life that are mentioned or implied in the Bible:

1. *Patriarchal* (father-ruled) *extended families*   Gen. 14:14
   including grandparents, servants, etc.: Abraham's
   household numbered 318 men, not counting women
   and children

2. *Polygamous marriage*: one man with several or   Deut. 21:15
   many wives and/or concubines and their children

3. *Monogamous husband and promiscuous wife:*   Hosea 1-3
   Hosea and Gomer

4. *Female-headed extended family:* Rahab and   Joshua 6:17, 25
   her household

5. *Matrilocal families:* Jacob and Moses lived for   Gen. 29-31
   long periods with the birth-families of their   Exod. 2:21-22
   wives

6. *Single parents* and their children:
   a widow and her two sons a   2 Kings 4:1-7
   widow and her resurrected son   Luke 7:11-12

7. *Levirate marriages:* a brother marrying the   Deut. 25: 5-10
   widow of his deceased brother   Matt. 22: 23-27

8. *Families in which the wife clearly held the prestige:*
   Lappidoth and Deborah, judge of Israel   Judges 4:4
   Nabal and Abigail, who saved the family by   1 Sam. 25:2-35
        placating King David after Nabal's rudeness
   Shallum and Huldah, a prophet consulted by   2 Kings 22:14ff
        the King of Judah

9. *Monogamous marriage* and the idea of   Gen. 2:24
   "one-fleshedness"   Matt. 19:5

10. *Same-sex partnerships:* (1) Naomi and Ruth,   Ruth 1:16-17
    later modified to an extended family in which
    Naomi was declared the mother of Ruth's son
    (2) the two disciples on the road to Emmaus who   Luke 24:29
    invited Jesus to "stay with us"

11. *"Trial marriages":*   among the Hebrews, sex   Exod. 21:8
    was not prohibited during the betrothal period,
    and even at weddings, the major ceremony was the
    sexual intimacy itself—cf. the Song of Solomon
    and the "premarital sex" of Ruth and Boaz, Ruth 3:7

12. *Unrelated adults sharing a home:* the widows who   Acts 9:36-39
    mourned Dorcas apparently lived in community

13. *Related single adults sharing a home:* Martha,   Luke 10:38-40
    Mary, and Lazarus: Luke 10:38 indicates that
    Martha headed the household

14. *Celibate singles—Jesus, John the Baptist, Paul (?)*

15. *Spiritual marriages:* a Christian man and "his   1 Cor. 7:36-38
    virgin" cohabiting except for sexual intimacy—
    an approved practice until the end of the fourth
    century

16. *A "homeless household":* Jesus   Matt. 8:20

17. *A Christian commune:* all property was held in   Acts 4:32
    common

18. *An equal-partners dual-career marriage:*   Acts 18:2-3,
    Priscilla and Aquila both traveled with Paul,   18, 26
    team-taught the Bible, and were tentmakers
    by trade

19. *Immigrant families:*
    Joseph to Egypt; family followed   Gen. 42-46
    Elimelech, Naomi, and their sons to Moab   Ruth 1:1-2

20. *Adoption within the extended family:* Hadassah (Esther) was adopted by her cousin Mordecai; Ephraim and Manasseh were adopted by their grandfather Jacob — Esther 2:15,20 / Gen.48:6

21. *Cross-cultural adoptive family:*
Moses was adopted by Pharaoh's daughter — Exod. 2:10
Believers are adopted into God's family — Rom. 8:14

22. *Cross-class adoptive family:* Eliezer, a slave born in Abraham's household, was adopted by Abraham — Gen.15:2-3

23. *Women living together in a harem* under the custody of a eunuch — Esther 2:3

24. *Cohabitation without marriage:* Samson and Delilah — Judges 16:4ff.

25. *Marriage in which sexual intimacy ceases* because of alienation: King David and Michal — 2 Sam. 6:16-23

26. *Nomad families living in tents* in the desert:
Jacob's family — Gen. 25:27 etc.
Israel's forty years of wandering — Num. 14:33 etc.

27. *Widow living with her parents:* Orpah — Ruth 1:8,14-15

28. *Divorced man in second marriage:* King Ahasuerus and Queen Esther, after Vashti was rejected — Esther 2:17

29. *Women married by force:* the daughters of Shiloh abducted by the Benjamites; and women taken as the spoils of war — Judges 21

30. *Surrogate motherhood:*
Hagar bore Ishmael for Abraham and Sarah — Gen. 16:1-15

Bilhah bore Dan and Naphtali for Jacob and Rachel   Gen. 30:1-7
Zilpah bore Gad and Asher for Jacob and Leah   Gen. 30:9-13

31. *Families established through incest:* Lot's   Gen. 19:31-38
    children conceived by his daughters

32. *Interracial/intercultural marriages:*
    Moses married Zipporah of Midian   Exod. 2:15-21
    Esau married two Canaanite wives   Gen. 27:46
    Ruth of Moab married Boaz of Israel   Ruth 4:9-10
    Ahasuerus, King of Medes and Persians,
        married Esther, a Jew   Esther 2:17
    Timothy had a Jewish mother and a Greek father   Acts 16:1-3

33. *Childless marriages:* Tamar's to Er and Onan   Gen. 38:6-10

34. *Blended families:* Jepthah was Gilead's son by a Judges 11:1-3
    harlot; Gilead's sons by his wife rejected
    Jepthah.
    Herod Antipas and Herodias (with Salome,   Luke 3:19
    Herodias's daughter by her previous marriage)

35. *"Commuter marriages":* Peter, traveling with   Matt. 8:14
    Jesus; his wife and her mother living at home
    Joana, wife of Chuza (Herod's steward), traveling Luke 8:3
    with Jesus

36. *Group living of people with physical or mental*   Luke 17:12
    disabilities

37. *Younger people caring for elderly people:*
    John and Mary, Jesus' mother   John 18:15-16
    Rufus and his mother   Rom. 16:13

38. *Religiously mixed marriages*   1 Cor. 7:12-16

39. *Unrelated people living in an ascetic religious* Matt. 19:11-12
    community; adopting children to perpetuate
    community: the Essenes

40. *Unrelated people traveling with Jesus,* supported   Luke 8:1-3
    by several of the women

© V. R. Mollenkott, 1991[3]

For the most part, these various family arrangements are mentioned without particular praise or condemnation. Yet some family types are more able to carry the covenantal one-flesh ideal than others.

Paul Eppinger notes at least five purposes of marriage in the Old Testament; at least the first four fall short of the one-flesh ideal. (1) In the patriarchal period, one purpose of marriage was to assure immortality to the male through the begetting of male children. (2) During the period of the monarchy, one purpose of marriage among royalty was to increase political power and form political alliances. Marriage was politically expedient. (3) The common citizen might have married for economic purposes. Several wives could bear many children to provide a work force. (4) Two prophets (Isaiah and Hosea) spoke of their marriages and seemed to see their families as extensions of their prophetic messages. (5) Returning from the exile, the leader Ezra saw that marriage maintained and perpetuated a covenant people.[4]

Rodney Clapp points out that the Old Testament includes a number of family practices that we neither can nor in most cases want to imitate. For example, the Israelite family could be polygamous. Further, these families did not divide private and public worlds; they existed as economic, agricultural, political, military units. There was no concept of nuclear family, but rather of households and clans, with rare exception headed by a male.

For the most part, Israelite families were unsentimental and non-romantic. Marriages represented covenants between two families even more than between two people; they were arranged, usually by fathers, to consolidate the strength and resources of the families involved. There might be romantic love in a marriage (it would usually come after the wedding), but it was not essential. (A notable exception was Jacob's love for Rachel. He labored fourteen years for her. See Gen. 29.)

In the Old Testament, there is a matter-of-fact depiction of the father's complete control over the disposal of his children. He could sacrifice them (Gen. 22; Judg. 11:34-40); sell them into slavery, concubinage (Exod. 21:7-11), or prostitution (Lev. 19:29 commands fathers not to do so); or have them executed (Deut. 13:6-9; 21:12-21; Gen. 38:24).[5]

Our most basic point is that throughout the biblical era there was much more diversity in families than one might think. There is also as much family diversity in the Bible as there is in contemporary culture.

Further, the difference between biblical families and our experience of family life today is greater than we often realize.

Divorce—In What Context?

The Bible includes frequent discussion of divorce. The entire biblical witness on divorce needs to be heard in context.

In the Bible divorce is mentioned in a wide variety of situations and literature. A few highlights: Legislative passages provide regulations around divorce. These may have to do with daughters of priests who have been divorced (Lev. 22:13); with women who have been seduced or slandered (Deut. 22:19, 28-29); or with the divorce process itself (Deut. 24:1-4).

In at least one setting, divorce is seen as necessary to sever ties with corrupting cultures and to call Israelites back to covenant and purity. The account is found in Ezra 10:11: "Separate yourselves from the peoples of the land and from the foreign wives." A religious leader of the day perceived God to be commanding divorce in that situation. The subsequent story indicates that the command was carried out.

In many passages the prophets used divorce as a metaphor to illustrate the relationship of God to the people of Israel. These include Jeremiah 3:1-8; Isaiah 50:1; and Hosea 1-3.

In at least one passage the prophet Malachi looked with alarm on the frequency of divorce he was seeing. He criticized men for deserting "the wife of your youth . . . though she is your companion and your wife by covenant. . . . For I hate divorce, says the Lord, the God of Israel" (Mal. 2:14, 16). This is one of the few places where discussion of marriage and divorce clearly connects with the ideal set forth in Genesis.

Taken together, this variety of biblical passages and teachings seems to indicate that divorce was a rather common practice. It was culturally acknowledged and common enough to be an easily recognized metaphor. Divorce required humanizing legislation and outraged sensitive prophetic voices.

The teaching and law around divorce (most notably Deut. 24:1-4)

moved in the direction of slowing down the divorce process and of protecting the rights of women, who had almost no power in that society.
While such legislation may have moved in that direction, male power
still dominated. Divorce was a male prerogative and could throw a woman into dire straits.

This brings us to Jesus' words on divorce. When asked about grounds
for divorce (how does one interpret Deut. 24:1-4, a hot topic on which
there was wide variety of opinion), Jesus refused to "bite." He didn't
discuss that passage at all, but rather directed them back to that founda-
tional biblical teaching about marriage, Genesis 2. Then he added, "So
they are no longer two, but one flesh. Therefore what God has joined together, let no one separate" (Matt. 19:6; see Matt. 19:3-12; Mark 10:2-12;
Matt. 5:32; Luke 16:18). Jesus saw marriage as a relationship where
"God has joined together." There is promise here—that God is in the
midst of our partnerships offering to bond us to each other, present to
sustain us in the hard times and comfort us when we are struggling with
each other. This relationship participates in the sacred, and so Jesus
added, "Therefore what God has joined together, let no one separate."
He was saying to the culture of his day—and ours—don't let the institutional practices of society compromise our best efforts and tear apart our
cherished relationships.

Jesus did allow that Moses permitted divorce "for the hardness of
your hearts." Sometimes marriages are a mistake; they are mismatches.
Relationships do harden, become brittle, destructive, and abusive. If
hearts have hardened, divorce should be sorrowfully permitted so that
healing may begin.

At least one passage from the apostle Paul should be mentioned. In
1 Corinthians 7:12-16, he advised believers married to unbelievers to
stay married if the unbeliever was willing. But if the unbeliever left, "the
brother or sister is not bound. It is to peace that God has called you" (v.
15).

What do we make of the teachings of Jesus and of Paul in the context
of the Old Testament heritage of teaching on marriage and divorce?
Clearly Jesus stood with the prophetic voices that had called for slowing,
challenging, and humanizing divorce. He called people back to obedience to God's original intent for marriage. That much is clear. What is
not clear is how to be respectful and obedient to these teachings.

Myrna and Robert Kysar suggest that a first step in dealing with

Jesus' teachings is to see two aspects of his teaching in dynamic tension with each other: (1) Jesus spoke of the *absolute will of God*, the *creative intent* of God. He called people to live life in anticipation of God's kingdom as children of the kingdom now, obedient in act, motivation, and heart. (2) Jesus also spoke of the *absolute love* of *God*, the *redemptive intent* of God. He modeled and lived out an acceptance of folks who could not live within traditional religious teaching, much less his radical ethic of the kingdom.

In some areas of life, the Gospels reveal both aspects of Jesus' teaching. In this area of divorce, for the most part we have only Jesus' statements of the first, the absolute will of God. At the same time we have at least one example of Jesus' living out the second aspect as well—his encounter with the much married woman of Samaria in John 4. Jesus did not blame the victim. Rather he looked directly at her circumstances with love and acceptance of the person. In so doing, he opened the door for her to be a powerful transparent witness to others.

Some interpret these biblical teachings by making them into a new legislation. People may not divorce or may divorce only for infidelity or nonfaith of a spouse. If believers divorce for reasons other than these, there may be consequences, such as expulsion from a given church.

Others neglect these teachings and act as if they never existed.

There is certainly a much more faithful way to understand these teachings. They were a call to repentance to people who had grown lax and flip about divorce. They were not a new law but an extraordinary ethical ideal. Jesus' whole ministry was an attack on legalism. Life in the reign of God of which Jesus spoke cannot be neatly packaged. To make these teachings into law (civic or ecclesiastical) does violence to the spirit of Jesus.[6]

We heartily concur with Richard Foster who notes, "What we must not do is to turn these perceptive words of Jesus about [divorce and] remarriage into another set of soul-killing laws."[7] Other ethical methods will need to be found to live out obedience to this body of biblical-theological teaching. There is a way to take these passages seriously and be true to their intent and spirit without resorting to legalism.

As a pastoral counselor (Dick) and as a church educator (Joe), we applaud and embrace counseling and educational strategies that strengthen marriages and help troubled couples reconcile. We believe there is much we can do to help people enter into marriage with realism and commitment. And we see a special need to aid in the marriage preparation of high-risk people, such as those with previous marriages.

Even so, sometimes, down the road, a divorce may be the best possible decision, given the alternatives. At this point help with grieving and achieving the separation in the least destructive way may be the caring Christian's appropriate response. These are ways we seek to be faithful to Jesus and his teachings on marriage and divorce. We will speak more on these matters in the next chapter.

Singleness Affirmed

In the New Testament, singleness is affirmed, praised, lived.

Jesus, John the Baptist, Paul, and others lived as single people. Jesus and Paul were born into a culture that saw marriage and child bearing as an expectation and a blessing. Indeed, in an era that did not have a clear belief in life after death, children were one's immortality. To be single and childless was to perish. Jesus inaugurated and Paul heralded a new age. Christ rose and was the first born among us all. Therefore, people could make new decisions, and the needs of the age could affect decisions about marriage, child bearing, and singleness.

Jesus and Paul modeled and taught that singleness can be an appropriate way to live. For some people in some situations, they said, it may well be the most fitting way to respond to the Gospel (see Matt. 19; 1 Cor. 7). As we will explore in more detail, Jesus radically proclaimed that no loyalty—including family loyalty—should take precedence over commitment to God's kingdom. For some, that basic commitment may mean remaining single. As a part of an alert readiness for Christ's return, Paul thought it wise for some to remain single.

The principle remains that singleness can be a most effective way of life in stressful times. It may be so at other times as well. For those whose work is all encompassing or demanding, for those whose responsibilities require much travel or living in treacherous environments, singleness may be especially fitting. A gift of singleness may be mobility. A gift of marriage may be hospitality. As Paul says in 1 Corinthians 7, either marriage or singleness might be one aspect of one's calling as Christian.

Rodney Clapp (to whom we are indebted for this discussion) goes on to suggest that single Christians may be our most radical witnesses to a variety of Christian freedoms. Among these are *freedom from biological compulsion*, the understanding that genital expression is something that can be and should be disciplined, consistent with one's purposes in life. They also witness to our *freedom to marry*. If one is not free to remain single, then marriage is not a freely chosen option. Further, they witness to the *freedom to be a whole self rather than a schizophrenic self*. They are people who, for a time at least, have made one clear identity choice from a variety of options. Then there is the *freedom to enjoy positive freedom* as well as negative freedom. The experience of singleness provides opportunity not only to claim freedom from something but freedom for something. And single Christians can claim the *freedom to acknowledge and live within limits*. The single has one set of limits, the married person and/or parent has another.

Whether one goes all the way with the argument just cited, one thing is clear. New Testament affirmation of singleness is an important component in a faith ethic for today. As Clapp puts it, "one sure sign of a defective interpretation of Christian family is that it denigrates and dishonors singleness."[8]

Idolatry of Family Challenged

In the Bible, idolatry of the family is challenged. The importance of the family is as means, not an end.

A number of Bible scholars have been revisiting New Testament teachings on the family, asking, "Is the Bible profamily?" The answer is not an unequivocal yes. If profamily means making the family the goal and end of everything, the answer is a clear no.

Occasionally Jesus approved the command to honor parents and supported the traditional Jewish family structure. See for example Matthew 19:16-22 and Luke 18:18-30. But actually Jesus had very little to say about the family.

Isabel Rogers notes that more typically and frequently, there was a challenge to a supreme loyalty to one's biological family. At age twelve the young Jesus seemed to be seeking a new "home"—the temple in Jerusalem.

In his ministry he repeatedly and clearly called for the highest loyalty to God. God will be served through a new community, a new family if you will. This may cause stress and strain for families:

- Jesus proclaimed a kingdom that would divide families. "I have come to set a man against his father, / and a daughter against her mother, . . . / and one's foes will be members of one's own house hold" (Matt. 10:35-36).

- Jesus made it clear that loyalty to himself must come before all other loyalties. "Whoever loves father or mother ... or son or daughter more than me is not worthy of me" (Matt. 10:37). He also spoke of the loyalties over family. "And everyone who has left houses or brothers or sisters or father or mother or children or fields, for my name's sake, will receive a hundredfold, and will inherit eternal life" (Matt. 19:29).

- Jesus lived out this commitment himself. His mother Mary went out to "restrain him, for people were saying, 'He has gone out of his mind'" (Mark 3:21). Mother and brothers arrived at a crowded place where Jesus was and sent in word of their presence. Jesus responded, "Whoever does the will of God is my brother and sister and mother" (Mark 3:35).

Mary came to Jesus as his mother, but Jesus said that her new place was as a disciple of the kingdom. One Bible scholar notes, "It's not that Jesus is repudiating family relationships, but he is re-defining them."9

In the rest of New Testament writings, there is also new definition of family. Among the early Christians, the *church* is the household of God, the first family, if you will.

Janet Fishburn points out how family language permeates the book of Ephesians, which in part accounts for its continuing appeal. People have come into this new community, Ephesians tells us, by "washing of water by the word" (5:26). God wants this Christian community to be as beautiful as the bride on the day of the wedding (5:27). God is named as the one "from whom every family in heaven and on earth takes its name" (3:15). Christians are described as members of the "household of God" (2:19).

Fishburn notes, "The writer of Ephesians uses the language of courtship and marriage to convey the passion and mystery of Christ's union with the church." The New Testament teaching reverses the common Protestant tradition that the "Christian home" should be a little church. Rather, the church, "the household of God" is a new, large family.

This leads Fishburn to a basic premise: "it is the church— and not a biological family unit—that is the first family of all baptized Christians." She notes further, "The biblical tradition affirms the family but limits its significance."[10]

In reflecting on this New Testament evidence, Rodney Clapp is led to two declarations, one negative, one positive.

> The negative declaration: The family is not God's most important institution on earth. The family is not the social agent that most significantly shapes and forms the character of Christians. The family is not the primary vehicle of God's grace and salvation for a waiting, desperate world.
>
> And the positive declaration: The church is God's most important institution on earth. The church is the social agent that most significantly shapes and forms the character of Christians. And the church is the primary vehicle of God's grace and salvation for a waiting, desperate world.[11]

By including this quotation, we are aware of a contradiction. At the beginning of chapter 1, we included a quote where Loren Mead, a theologian of the church, says that the human family is the most important source of meaning and community. Here Rodney Clapp, a theologian of the family, says the church is God's most important institution. While we feel Clapp overstates his case, the strain between these two claims feels creative. It partakes of Christian paradox. In the tension of the importance of these two significant agencies—church and family—a theological ethic for family begins to take form.

Today's emphasis on the isolated family unit and on the individual leads to these assumptions: God (and God's sovereign reign) exist for the church, which exists for the family, which exists for the individual.

The scholars of whom we speak turn this paradigm around: The individual exists for the family, which exists for the church, which exists for God and God's sovereign reign. Or perhaps all of these entities exist for mutual service to all the others. We do not exist for ourselves—

individual people or families—we exist for God's family and ultimately for God, in whose will is our peace.

There is reassurance here. God has created two institutions and entrusted great responsibility to each. The responsibilities are not the same but are complementary. Families are for reproduction, for sex, for mutual guidance, for sustaining people in their need for intimacy. Churches are places where there is intimacy of a different kind, where we bond in mission, where we consciously and corporately keep in touch with transcendence and eschatological hope, and where our family and other relationships are tested with reality checks and serious encounters with the Word. Sometimes the church compensates for bad family life. Sometimes family life compensates for inadequate church experience. Sometimes church and family reinforce each other in healthy, productive, and faithful ways.

There are also some warnings here. First, beware of making one's own family one's god. Do not let the family be your highest or only focus of loyalty, and do not let it be your ultimate security.

Second, leaders must avoid making "ministry to families" an end in itself without at the same time empowering "ministry with families" and "ministry from families."

Third, one should avoid elevating a particular family form to sacred status. Some Christian leaders have seen the nineteenth-century, middle-class, patriarchal family as what God has ordained for all families. If that is the view, any decrease or deviation from it causes alarm. However, both Scripture and intercultural studies reveal that God has many ways for families to carry on their lives together. Within a new awareness of New Testament teachings about family, there is a relief of old burdens and a call to be a part of a new reality.

Vision of Mission

Out of this, there emerges an exciting, empowering vision of the mission, the vocation of Christian families.

While the family may not be as central or as ultimate as some have thought it to be, families do have a vital part in the divine economy. God has a purpose (or purposes) for families.

Consider the family's mission in the New Testament church. Peter Lampe has noted a number of aspects of this mission.

One task was to provide a location for Christian gatherings. The New Testament speaks of "the church in your house" (Philem. 1:2). There were no church buildings, so "churches" were groups as large as could meet in one home, perhaps twenty to thirty. This small-group style could encourage personal contacts, frequent interaction, affectionate community. There was no room for anonymity. The "house church" was a powerful tool in guiding/incorporating new believers. Families with a large enough home to host a small church rendered a valuable service indeed.

Yet another family opportunity was to provide hospitality for traveling missionaries and evangelists. It was also hoped that the family's style of life would attract pagan neighbors to a hunger for the Gospel.

Still another family mission was the raising and instructing of its own children in the Christian faith. Quite likely, there was no specific churchwide instruction for children. This was the responsibility of both father and mother. If the children were fortunate enough to receive education outside the home, it was entirely secular. "In sum, the Christian household was about the only place where a child could be taught the Christian tradition and values in ways a child could grasp."[12]

There was an even more basic mission for Christian families; they were to be a model for the local and indeed the universal church. The family modeled, taught, and thus provided "categories for the formulation of theology, ecclesiology and ethics."[13]

Here we see the family's great dignity and significance. The nature of family relationships and the quality of family life provide ways to think about theology. The family also serves as a sign that universal church is possible.

Family language describes salvation and church community. God is parent. Jesus is the first born among many siblings. Through Jesus, the first born, we are adopted into the family of God. We are called to use our varied skills to build up the household of God. As parents are committed to their children throughout their lifetimes, nothing will separate us from the love of God, as expressed in the first born, Jesus Christ our Lord.

The family symbols are not always consistent. While sometimes Christ is the brother, at other times he is the husband, the groom. The church collectively becomes the bride.

In the New Testament writers speak of theology using family terms. The theological categories of God, Christ, salvation, and the sociological categories of father, mother, child, husband, and wife enrich one another. Families are called to be living expressions of the theological truth as well as the means by which it is understood.

In the discussion of marriage starting with Ephesians 5:21, for example, marriage guidance and teaching about the Gospel intersect. Husbands and wives are told to "Be subject to one another out of reverence for Christ." Wives are then told to relate to their husbands as the church, the bride, relates to Christ (or should). Husbands are called to be sacrificial as Christ was for the church. The writer then quotes the classic marriage text, Genesis 2, "For this reason a man will leave his father and mother and be joined to his wife, and the two will become one flesh" (Eph. 5:31). The writer goes on to say that this is a great mystery, which he takes to be referring to Christ and church, but he concludes with a summary call to mutual respect for husbands and wives.

In Ephesians 6 the writer goes on to speak of the relationship between children and parents. Children are told to obey, and thus to participate in divine commandment and receive of its promises. Parents are urged not to be so harsh as to turn children from faith, but "bring them up in the discipline and instruction of the Lord" (v. 4).

A confused outsider might ask, "Are you discussing theology, or are you giving family guidance?" The answer would be "Yes! Families are only a part of the redemptive story, but they are a most significant part."

Families have a related calling in the present day and age. They also have many problems and issues with which to contend. In the next chapter we will outline five basic ministries of the church that address these quandaries and the callings facing families.

CHAPTER 4

Supporting Families in the Congregation

Family ministry is not a "new" ministry, something "extra" for the church which can afford it, the last program to be added when the worship and Bible study and music program are in place. . . . The challenge for congregations, therefore, is to adopt family ministry as a perspective from which to view the entire life and activity of the congregation, not just those programs that carry content readily identifiable as "family."

—Diana Garland[1]

In the previous chapter, we described the ethical model of a round-table dialogue of four equal partners: Scripture and theological reflection; personal experience; discoveries from social science research; and the wisdom of the church. We wove together information and guidance from each of those sources, with a primary focus on the Bible. Now as we turn to practical strategies for ministry, our ethical reflection will draw more on the other three partners.

We approach this part of our discussion in the pastoral spirit of 1 Corinthians 7:25, "I have no command of the Lord, but I give my opinion as one who by the Lord's mercy is trustworthy." You in turn will need to measure the directions we suggest by your own reliable opinion in your particular setting. *You* complete the round table, bringing the wisdom of your church and personal experience to the issues challenging families in your care that cry out for ethical wisdom and practical ministry.

Our purpose in this book is to sketch out a new paradigm for families and for ministries with families. One part of the new paradigm is our understanding that families are social systems rather than simply collections of individuals. Another part of the new paradigm is our understanding that economic and social forces are shaping a greater diversity of family configurations. This paradigm shift in understanding families requires a shift in the way we organize ministries with families. Sketching that shift is the task we set before us in this chapter.

Supporting Family Systems

As systems, families have rules by which they operate, patterns of authority and power, rituals, and decision-making processes. Family units have needs, aspirations, and goals. Elise Boulding speaks of "family agenda," arising out of family interaction, that is acted out in the world beyond the family by family members. She notes that considerable social change at the grassroots level is generated by the conversation, planning, and identification of needs and goals as part of the ordinary flow of daily family living. Public causes arise out of "private" family interactions.[2]

For example, looking at new towns that sprang up in the west during the energy boom of the seventies, Boulding was able to show that the development of community institutions (libraries, children's sports leagues, musical organizations, day-care centers, civic betterment organizations) flowed from the process in family households of identifying goals and needs. Family members giving leadership in the community were in fact carrying out family agenda developed through the process of family interaction.

Of course families are not always successful in achieving their goals or meeting their needs. In earlier chapters we have identified many of the stresses on families today and the fall-out in disrupted relationships. To survive the stresses on them, families require support. They require support to become centers of wholeness in which intimate relationships thrive. Families must be supported by a network of other families, institutions, and community practices if they are to be successful in nurturing the next generation. The concept of family support underlies our new paradigm in family ministry.

The term *family support* involves ministering with families in a way that puts them in charge of the care or services they are receiving. It involves respecting the needs, aspirations, and goals families have identified, rather than imposing your pastoral care or programs on them. It means offering care or programs based on deep regard for families' stated wishes and priorities. To minister within a framework of family support means two things: (1) *listening to what families say* about their lives, hopes, and needs; and (2) *believing in the capacity of Christians to reach out to one another* in powerfully caring ways. It means structuring places and times when families can give one another support and care.3

We recognize that congregations do more than simply support families; we have no quarrel with the need for congregations to pursue their evangelical and missional objectives. But if congregations want to be effective in family ministry today, they need to consider a family support approach. The new paradigm for family ministries is to discover, invent, or develop support strategies that deal with issues families identify as priority. It is the opposite of adding yet more programs into which families must fit.

Supportive Listening

The first step in this approach is listening. For example, a church leader might sit down with two or three single parents and invite them to tell their stories; this conversation can identify the needs these families consider priority. Inviting a couple married for decades to speak in a worship service, telling how God has been present in their relationship, can highlight for a whole congregation some of the supportive ingredients that sustain enduring partnerships. If the congregation sponsors a day-care center or nursery school, meeting with a group of parents and a teacher can bring to light the concerns, hopes, and obstacles faced by younger families today.

There is simply no substitute for inviting families to reflect on their experiences with you and speak of their goals, needs, and hopes. Armed with the living data from such interactions, leaders can craft worship services, educational programs, enrichment opportunities, and discipleship and support groups that will enable families to find in the congregation many of the resources they need.

Conviction for Reaching Out

The second step in helping a congregation become a family-supportive body is *believing in the willingness and capacity of Christian people to reach out to one another*. This conviction is rooted in a Christian under-standing of community. "They'll know we are Christians by our love" says a well-known song. It suggests that the spirit of Christian commu-nity is embodied in acts of mutuality. Your need is my opportunity for ministry, and vice versa. The basis for Christian community is our needi-ness, our deepest hopes and aspirations. It is around precisely the stuff of family agenda that we can be united in Christ with each other.

It is striking that half the U.S. population participates in small self-help groups. Thousands of men are gathering each summer in football stadiums to encourage one another to be "promise keepers," responsible husbands and fathers. The search for community marks our ever more impersonal society. And the church knows deep in its bones about com-munity! In his letters Paul admonishes the churches to practice mutual-ity, to level the social hierarchy imposed by secular society, to establish accountable person-to-person and family-to-family relationships. An active belief in the capacity of Christians to be primary supports to one another is key to developing effective family ministries.

Armed with the concept of family support and the conviction that Christians will reach out to one another, we dare to believe that every congregation, large or small, can make a difference in the quality of family life experienced by its members. This chapter outlines five basic dimensions of family ministry and offers practical strategies. We believe every congregation *can:*

- create a family-friendly culture in its own life and in the surrounding community;
- help families identify their unique missions as members of the larger household of God;
- equip families to be enriching communities for each member;
- strengthen the commitment of couples to their marriage/partnership covenants;
- develop a theology of singleness and ministries of respect, inclusion, and support for single adults.

1. Seek a Family-Friendly Culture

The first dimension of a congregation's family ministry is to *seek a culture—including church, workplace, government, and media—that is more family friendly.*

In *The Once and Future Church*, Loren Mead speaks of three paradigms for the relationship of church to world and culture. In the early centuries an apostolic church paradigm applied. The church lived in a hostile, persecuting atmosphere. In the next paradigm, the age of Christendom (following Constantine's conversion), church and empire were seen virtually as one. The church existed in an extremely supportive environment. An American version of Christendom existed at least to the middle of the twentieth century, but then crumbled. A new paradigm is emerging, the form of which is not yet entirely clear, not for church, not for family.

Mead speaks of the ambiguous culture in which the church now lives—sometimes hostile, sometimes supportive, sometimes neutral, sometimes pushing church to the boundaries of triviality. Families also live in that ambiguous environment. As we seek to keep the faith within our culture, we need to name, identify, and analyze aspects of it that are unfriendly, even harmful, to families. We are also called to stand at the side of families damaged by particular cultural conflicts or distortions, offering them aid and support. Further we will have the double opportunity/responsibility of (1) creating countercultural styles and (2) working to influence the culture to be more family friendly.

How Family Friendly Is Your Community?

Some communities welcome families with children: the parks have play equipment; the buses easily accommodate toddlers in strollers; the schools schedule parent conferences at times when parents can actually attend; at least some churches offer worship services in which children can participate; in congregations seniors have opportunities to grandparent the community's children.

Other communities make it clear they are only for certain kinds of families. We're all familiar with retirement communities in which overnight guests under eighteen are not allowed. Not all signals are so extreme.

Does your community offer day care that a single mother can afford? Are there after-school activities for young people? Will landlords rent to a biracial couple or to two women and their children? Will a congregation welcome them? Do doctors in your community accept Medicaid cards? Is there a Parents' Anonymous hotline offering help any time a parent at the end of his or her resources needs it?

What Research Shows

Whether children growing up in families thrive or fail to thrive depends on both formal programs and informal supports that nurture family wholeness. In fact research demonstrates that congregations offering ministries to young people and their families make a major difference in the well-being of both.

The Search Institute is dedicated to promoting the positive development of children and youth through research and development of practical resources. Between September 1989 and March 1990, the institute conducted a comprehensive study of 47,000 young people in grades six through twelve from 111 mainly Midwestern communities. The sample was racially and ethnically inclusive, although 90 percent of the student respondents were identified as White.[4]

When compared, this sample of largely "middle America" youth and other available representative national data (on measures such as alcohol and tobacco use, sexual abuse, involvement in extracurricular activities, and exposure to television) showed remarkably similar results. We are comfortable applying the findings of this study to almost any community in the United States.

Search Institute based its survey on the interaction of three important variables. First, they measured the *assets* in the lives of young people. These included *psychological support* (offered by family, good parent communication, positive school climate), *control* (parental discipline, monitoring, positive peer influence), *structured time use* (involvement in school extracurricular activities such as athletics or music, involvement in church or synagogue), *educational commitment* (achievement motivation, educational aspiration, homework), *positive values* (committed to helping people, sexual restraint, caring about others' feelings), and *social competence* (assertiveness skills, friendship-making skills, self-esteem).

Second, the study assessed the *deficits* in the lives of youth. Deficits include being *alone at home* (two hours or more a day without an adult), *hedonistic values* (high importance placed on self-serving), *TV overexposure* (three or more hours per day), *drinking parties* (frequent attendance at parties where peers drink), *stress* (feels under pressure most or all of the time), *physical abuse* (reports at least one incident of abuse by an adult), *sexual abuse* (reports at least one incident), *parental addiction* (reports that parent has serious problem with alcohol or drugs), *social isolation* (feels consistent lack of care, support, understanding), and *negative peer pressure* (most close friends involved in chemical use or in trouble at school).

Third, nearly all youth at some point engage in *at-risk behaviors*. These are related to *alcohol* (frequent alcohol use, binge drinking), *tobacco* (daily cigarette use, frequent chewing-tobacco use), *illicit drugs* (use six or more times in last year), *sexuality* (sexual activity and nonuse of contraceptives), *depression/suicide* (reports depression and/or attempts at suicide), *antisocial behavior* (vandalism, group fighting, police trouble, theft, weapon use), *school* (absenteeism, desire to drop out), *vehicle safety* (driving and drinking, riding and drinking, seat belt nonuse), and other (for example, eating disorders).

The dramatic Search Institute findings demonstrated that the more assets and fewer deficits in the life of a young person, the fewer at-risk behaviors he or she is likely to exhibit. For all youth, the number of at-risk behaviors increases with age, regardless of family configuration.

Generally, youth from single-parent families are provided fewer assets than youth in two-parent families. Consequently, as just about every other survey of adolescents has shown, youth from single-parent households tend to engage in more at-risk behaviors than youth from two-parent homes. The difference in assets between two-parent and single-parent families accounts for much of the difference in at-risk behavior patterns. When single-parent homes provide nearly as many assets as two-parent homes, the youth in these families thrive!

Most exciting to us is the finding that the network of support a family enjoys, whether parented by one adult or two, is critical. When specific assets, such as high-quality schools, positive friends, involvement in extracurricular organizations, and involvement in religious institutions, are present in the lives of young people, they do well. Youth who grow up in single-parent homes and thrive (engage in no or one at-risk behavior) are twice as likely to have these specific assets in their lives as youth who do not thrive (exhibit five or more at-risk behaviors). Similarly, youth who thrive in spite of families that abuse substances or people are twice as likely to have these assets in their lives as nonthriving youth from similar homes.

The support network of church and community services and programs available to young people and their families makes an enormous difference in whether a youngster will be healthy or a statistic. Even two-parent homes do not produce thriving youngsters without the presence of support in the form of programs, ministries, and services. In the midst of the increasingly polarized and politicized discussion of the advantages of a two-parent home for a young person, it is worth keeping this perspective in view. Congregational support of families, through such "traditional" efforts as a youth program, can make all the difference to the well-being of the next generation!

Implications for Family Ministries

Beginning with strategies to make the congregation more family friendly, we offer these practical directions for ministry.

Respect a Family's Agenda

Families come to church with an agenda. They are often looking for specifics when they visit a congregation: Will this congregation provide a positive peer environment for my teenager? Will this congregation accept our member with disabilities? As a blended family, how will our children fit in to the church school? Will the teacher understand why it is important for my child to make two Mother's Day cards? Is there anything for newlyweds in this congregation? As a single dad, I wonder if the youth leaders will understand that my boy is with me only every other weekend. Is there an active couples' group in this congregation? I'm single and plan to remain that way; can I be a significant part of this congregation if I come without a partner? How open is this church to dealing with my adolescent daughter struggling with anorexia nervosa? I'm divorced; will that bar me from contributing as a teacher in the church school? We've just learned that our grandson is gay and has AIDS; can we let this be known here?

Today it is clear that families "shop" for congregations that fit their agenda. And families remain in congregations where their families' agenda are acknowledged and where it is easy to stay in touch with others who have similar goals or needs. This is an important question to ask: Does your congregation's life compete with or undergird the life of families that belong to it? That is a central issue raised by the new paradigm of family ministries we are suggesting. It might be helpful to inventory your congregation's life and program with these questions in mind:

- Where is it providing support to family relationships?
- Where is it thwarting family relationships?
- What family oriented content is offered in the worship, education, and outreach of our congregation?
- Do we provide experiences with an intergenerational focus as well as a peer group focus?
- Do our church programs put power in the hands of families to work at their own agenda?

Grow a Family-Friendly Climate at Church

A family-friendly climate in a congregation allows all kinds of families to feel comfortable. The Sunday morning greeters are not fazed when a new family visits and the surnames of the children are different. The way to the crib room or nursery is easy to find. The single mother and children are welcomed by pastor and church school teachers with the same enthusiasm as a two-parent family arriving in a van with two children and signs of a family dog.

In a family-friendly congregation, leaders in worship are both male and female, single and married, of many ages. Those who light the Advent candles or perform musically or usher represent many family configurations. God is invoked as more than "Father," as the rich variety of scriptural images of God are plumbed for their spiritual power. In artwork on bulletins, in Sunday school literature, and in the adornment of the building, a variety of human relationships are portrayed as "family."

A family-friendly congregation "does church" in ways that include all kinds of families. Take volunteer recruitment, for example. Traditional assumptions about which gender will do which jobs in the church no longer hold. The two-income pattern for two-parent families means that mother is not necessarily more available than dad for church-related activities. That makes fathers equal-opportunity volunteers! A family-friendly congregation does not assume that mothers only will staff the crib room. Fathers are just as available and, from what is known about fathering, just as capable. Congregations have found that short-term volunteer assignments (for a month, a quarter, a half-year) also seem to fit the commitment capacity of time-short family members.

Take the scheduling of church functions. When single-parent or blended families share custody of children with another household, you can expect children to be in church on something less than a regular weekly basis. Consideration of their needs might lead to youth events scheduled on week nights or to youth ministry organized around periodic retreats, with dates set well in advance so family schedules can be arranged. An awareness of children's bedtimes may mean scheduling earlier evening meetings or programs, perhaps with a meal, so families can still have some "wind-down time" at home before bed. Few congregations these days need to schedule meetings "after the milking is finished."

Church functions that offer prepared meals are especially welcoming to households where all the adults work outside the home and have little time to prepare casseroles for church suppers. Being able to gather the children or pick up grandmother and head for the church or come straight from work is a boon for families juggling two work schedules and single parents whose days are crammed full.

Family-friendly churches have learned to "network" households facing similar issues. In large congregations a hospitality committee might make sure families with compatible agenda meet one another. In smaller churches a pastor or lay leader might take on the responsibility to ask:

- the "veteran" widow to give a call to the new widow;
- the divorced mom who is doing well to seek out a recently divorced mom;
- the family with a year-old first child to be in touch with the family who has a newborn.

To "network" families, a person or group needs to be responsible for enhancing the quality of congregational life. The task is not a programmatic one; it is a ministry of making connections among folks. It is a ministry of alertness to the needs and goals of all kinds of families and sharing that awareness. In this way a congregation can create responsive programs and develop informal family supports.

Many computer-equipped congregations are finding a data base software increasingly helpful in networking and planning efforts. Such a package makes it easy to record notes about the needs, goals, and situations of individual families. When a particular need arises or a family encounters a major crisis or developmental milestone, families with similar agenda can be connected. A church planning group considering a new program or reshaping an old one can refer to this information about the real needs of people.

For example, Bill, a single young adult, expressed the desire to be part of a men's group. Existing men's groups in the congregation had formed around the issues facing middle-aged and older men. By accessing the church's data base, the church could easily identify Bill's peers in the congregation, making the search for other men with a similar interest much quicker and more productive.

Be a Family Advocate

Let's say a family asks the church for financial aid. The gas and electricity company is about to turn off the utilities for lack of payment. A caring church leader locates some church funds and helps the family find other finances from community resources. The family is then referred to the credit counseling agency in the community and to another family that lives simply within a similar income. This second family helps the first to learn new living strategies. Under loving but firm guidance, they cut up their credit cards and make small but steady progress on their debts. Eventually these and other families lobby and give public testimony on issues around too much and too easy credit.

There are many things a congregation can do to be more family friendly. Challenging the community to be family friendly is an important contribution. Being an advocate for families in your community may be a new role, but do not underestimate the impact you can have. Consider surveying your community to determine the ways it is family friendly and family unfriendly.

Take an inventory of the assets in your community that support families, using the work of the Search Institute as a guide.

- Are there after-school activities for young people in which they have an opportunity to interact with committed and trustworthy adults and with one another?

- Do schools offer support for high aspirations, have great expectations of their students, and offer a wide range of extracurricular activities to engage the minds and spirits of their students?

- What kinds of child care are offered and how much is available at an affordable price?

- Do local media take note of couples celebrating fifty years together?

- Are families that are making it in spite of challenges lifted up in the local newspaper?

- Are older adults involved with children through school or day-care programs?

- What are families' perceptions of community acceptance of chidren?

When you have developed answers to these kinds of questions, publish your findings in the local media. Go on the cable station and talk about "how life is" for families in your neighborhood or town. Write an op-ed piece about it for the paper. Hold a community forum to share your findings and invite a panel of business, educational, and political leaders to attend and respond.

Sometimes advocacy simply means being available and hospitable. Offer your space to groups that support families with special needs, for example local chapters of Parents without Partners, the Step Family Association, Parents and Friends of Lesbians and Gays. Don't forget local or informal support groups for parents of children with disabilities, associations for infertile couples or adoptive families, Alcoholics Anonymous,

Adult Children of Dysfunctional Families, and so on. Consider starting support groups when they do not exist.

Advocacy lends itself to an ecumenical approach. Perhaps the council of churches (or equivalent group) in your community would be willing to sponsor a family advocacy task force. Such a group could commit itself to identifying issues of importance for supporting healthy families and raising community awareness about them.

A significant ecumenical strategy of support to homeless families has emerged in more than twenty states across the country: The Interfaith Hospitality Network (IHN).[5] Participating congregations in a locality band together to provide shelter, food, child care, and counseling to homeless families. Typically a small group of homeless families (meaning parents and children) is housed overnight for a week at a time in a congregation's space. At the end of the week, the families move on to the next congregation's facility. A central location is found where day care, employment counseling, case management services, bathing facilities, parent education programs, job training classes, and the like can be provided during the day. Hosting congregations (where families are housed) are joined by supporting congregations to provide an evening meal and hospitality volunteers who help with meals, play with children, visit with parents, and stay with the families overnight. IHN chapters do public education about homelessness and advocate for public policies to end the scandal of homelessness in America.

Other issues call for public advocacy by the religious community. Congregations might well advocate for a minimum wage that can support a family above the poverty level. Media issues may need to be addressed. For example, a congregation might monitor the levels of violence and portrayal of irresponsible sexuality on the programs offered by local channels and notify the station, its sponsors, and the newspaper of its findings and assessments. Another advocacy issue might be making the workplace more family friendly, even challenging the church as employer to live up to its rhetoric. An African proverb states, "It takes a village to raise a child." It's worth asking different parts of our culture to stop making it so difficult to raise a child!

2. See Family Life as Base for Mission

Consider a second dimension of family ministry: Stir a lively awareness of family life, not as an end in itself, but as a base for mission.

As we noted in chapter 3, families had a mission in New Testament times, and they still exist for mission today.

Rodney Clapp points out how self-defeating it becomes if families live only for themselves—when they go to church or engage in spiritual disciplines because it will strengthen the family. This is backwards. He writes:

> "The family that prays together, stays together" is not such an inno-
> cent statement. It is in fact just one more way to pervert both the
> church and the Gospel according to the dictates of the economic
> exchange model. If we worship and pray to God because that will
> strengthen our family, then we make worship and prayer (and God)
> into investment techniques that serve our ends. And ironically, the
> family hurts itself when it makes the family the goal and object of
> Christian mission and spiritual disciplines.[6]

The search needs to be for the family's broader mission, in support of and supported by other families.

One Family's Mission

In the title of their book, James and Kathleen McGinnis clearly articu-
late the mission for which their family lives: *Parenting for Peace and
Justice: Ten Years Later.*[7] Four aspects of their family commitment to
mission are especially noteworthy.

First, they speak of goals and strategies in the area of stewardship
and simple living. As a family they seek simplicity and health in their
diet, recreation, and use of money and energy. Recycling and making
contributions to causes chosen by family consensus are important strategies for them.

A second aspect is the practice of nonviolence in their family. They
use family meetings, nonviolent communication skills, and other strategies of conflict resolution. They also attempt to help their children deal

with violence in the world, including the war mentality and violence in
the media.

Third, the McGinnis family nurtures an awareness of the multicultural richness of the human family. They adopted a child from another
culture, and through the people, experiences, and resources they bring
into their lives, they seek to celebrate God's creative diversity. At the
same time they seek a nonsexist family life, by using inclusive language,
by doing tasks and enjoying activities without gender restrictions, and by
encouraging one another's internal qualities.

Finally, they invite total family involvement in social action when-
ever possible, though without forcing it or turning off their children by
undue pressure.

In a "ten years later" revision of their earlier book, the McGinnises
note that their children have grown from being preschool and grade
school children to adolescents. Their own parental strategies have had
to change, as did the children's amount of involvement. They sense that
some parts of their vision more than others have distilled in their children. By the time of the revision, they have taken on a new responsibility, for Kathy's aging parents. Whatever its form, their mandate to mission still holds.

The McGinnises are to be applauded for their vision, their transpar-
ency in attempting to live it, and the resources they provide others who
would share the journey. They quickly admit that they don't have the
only vision for family mission.

As part of its mission a family may work to strengthen an aspect of
its church's life—music or youth ministry or the nursery. Dick happened
upon part of his family mission when he took a small daughter with him
on pastoral calls to elderly members of his congregation. Finding this
fascinating and enriching, she wanted to go repeatedly. Now an adult,
she is a geriatric social worker, a vocation that is an extension of that
family mission she helped to formulate as a child. Joe came to part of his
family mission when special-needs children were born to Ginny and him.

Helping Families Discover Their Mission

Family mission may take many forms. It has to do with any children born
to the family, their present and future; it has to do with the family not

being simply a passive recipient of social change but an agent of social change; it has to do with family resources. Each family needs to discern and develop its own unique mission. This stands at the heart of a family-ministry strategy.

The congregation has a role to play in helping families discover their mission. Diana Garland, editor of the *Journal of Family Ministry*, reminds us that congregations can provide "an alternative ecology for family living."[8]

By this she means promoting covenantal relationships among church families that focus on practical matters, such as sharing expensive but necessary equipment and services including automobiles and child care. She envisions families reclaiming their productive functions through co-operative strategies that relieve the economic pressures on families and enable parents to spend more time caring for and educating their children in keeping with Christian values. Her call is to confront directly the barriers to meaningful and enduring relationships thrown up by contemporary social and cultural conditions. She challenges congregations to ask some searching questions:

- What would it take for parents to spend more quality time with their children?
- What do couples need so they can get away together and spend time on their relationship?
- Where does our voice need to be heard on behalf of families?
- How can a Christian community restructure itself so that supporting families is at the heart of its ministry?

Families will find their lives enriched and even transformed by participating in mission projects. A woman in Joe's church shared this story: "Al and I have a traditional division of labor. He cares for the garden, outside maintenance, and critters. I care for the inside, cooking, cleaning, critters. Wherever the children are, that parent is in charge. Recently I went to El Salvador with a women's delegation, leaving the family well supplied with prepared meals and the promise of Grandma's visits. Since I returned, Al has been doing dishes. He commented, 'My hands are no more holy than yours.'"

A family's crisis can sometimes be its call to family mission. In Dick's congregation a couple lost their six-year-old to meningitis. The relative rarity of a young child's death can be expected to have a heavy impact on a congregation as well as the family. Shortly another couple in the congregation delivered a still-born baby. Their chief comforters turned out to be the family grieving their own child.

While it is not reasonable or appropriate to expect that every deeply wounded family will be healers in a congregation, by the grace and Spirit of God, it does happen. A congregation can be open to the possibility. Families do find in unusually challenging experiences a call to mission. Often acting on that call is central to their own healing.

Implications for Family Ministry

Educational Strategies

One way to help families discover their mission is to develop a congregational expression of the Parenting for Peace and Justice Network (PPJN).[9] We've mentioned this group, above. Adult and intergenerational educational materials available through PPJN can spark the imagination of families. The Building Caring Families project of PPJN offers a way to combine family support groups with an educational process for discerning a family's call. This project provides a congregation with educational materials, leadership training, and two years of consultation. It is structured ecumenically so that congregations in a locality can network in support of families.

Discernment Strategies

Congregations can help families clarify their missions by offering discernment times or "clearness meetings." The basic idea, adapted from the Quaker tradition, is that the congregation (or a smaller representative group) can help a family think through an impending decision or opportunity for mission. For example, a couple considering living together or getting married might ask a group of fellow believers who know them well to gather in a clearness meeting to help them think through their decision. The couple would briefly relate some background about the decision they need to make. Then the members of the meeting would ask open-ended questions that push the couple to reflect on their motivations, the consequences of their decision, the alternatives open to them, and so on. The question period may take a half hour to forty-five minutes.

Following the questions, the couple may share their feelings about the experience and invite members of the group to do the same. The meeting may well end in corporate prayer for clarity about God's will. The purpose of the meeting is not to make the decision for the family but to help them get clearer about the dimensions of the decision facing them. The process lends itself to all kinds of family decisions: whether to adopt a child, take a new job, separate or divorce, enter or return to school, join a mission group.

Family Mission Projects

A congregation may also help families catch a vision of their mission through church mission projects and exchange projects. The experience of making preparations, perhaps traveling, and working together to accomplish a specific goal bonds one family with others and strengthens relationships within families. Habitat for Humanity projects are one readily available avenue for both local and long-distance mission work. Some of the activities already mentioned, such as serving homeless families, lend themselves to intergenerational involvement. There is unique teaching power in the experience of a parent and child helping someone in deep need.

We also recommend connecting families with student exchange programs. Student exchange programs enable families to use the gift of hospitality. In the process, they learn about another culture and connect with another family whose life situation may be quite different from theirs. Rural-urban exchange programs also help families cross boundaries and broaden their understanding.

3. Enrich Family Life

A church can and should make every effort to help the family be an enriching community for each member.

While we are committed to the concept of the families as means, and not only ends, there is another word to be said: Part of the church's mission is to help the family be a safe, caring, redemptive, healing place. Many turn to the church for precisely this kind of help. People will be grateful to the congregation that:

- has a vision as to what their family can be;
- protects and advocates for families;
- boldly confronts abusive behavior and helps deliver families from such destructive patterns;
- offers insight and information about family matters, including support, advice, and training;
- helps families become all they aspire to be.

The Family Needs to Be a Safe Place

The church needs to make every effort to eliminate abuse and violence of every form from every child and every spouse. This is first of all a preventive, educational task. Making clear that physical and sexual abuse is never right under any circumstances is the clear duty of church leaders. We have a solemn obligation to eliminate the notion that the Bible condones beating children or that wives are duty bound to submit to whatever their husbands demand or do.

Second, church leaders have an obligation to provide sanctuary to the victims of abuse. Clergy must understand that the safety of family members is the highest priority when domestic violence occurs. Sending a beaten wife or child back home "for the sake of the family" or "to preserve a marriage" can be fatal. Involving child protective services in the case of child abuse is at least a moral duty even where it is not a legal one for pastors and pastoral counselors.

Third, in terms of family, a theological task falls to the church. Sexism runs deep in our culture. Confronting the idea that men's role is to control and possess "their" women and children is a central part of what it means today to proclaim our creation as human beings in God's image.

The Family Needs to Be a Reliable Place

Children need to know consistently what behavior is allowed and what behavior is expected. One damaging aspect of families with an alcoholic member, for example, is that the home can be a loving, supportive place one day, and an erratic, destructive place the next. Similar unpredictability may occur in homes where a member suffers from mental illness. But of course people not struggling with alcoholism or mental illness may also prove inconsistent. Children—and all family members—have need for predictability and reliability in their home base.

Families Need to Be Economically Secure

There is a base economic level below which a family cannot function in a healthy way. The church should respond to individual family need and advocate for economic programs for families below that base.

A Vision of Healthy Family Life

All family types can be healthy and health giving. While single-parent families may have much heavier demands on adults and often fewer economic resources, they still have potential to be healthy families. Churches need to overcome the temptation to make married couples with children the norm. All family types with or without partners, with or without children, can be healthy and health giving.

Families need to be intentional about their life together, aware of what nurtures them, and committed to strengthening those aspects. Family researcher Virginia Satir contributed to this understanding, identifying a consistent pattern in her experience with optimally functioning families. (By this she meant families that are relatively untroubled, vital, and nurturing.) She identified four aspects of healthy family life: self-worth, communication, rules, and link to society.

In healthy families the individual members have a high sense of self-worth. Communication is honest, clear, direct, and specific. The family rules are flexible, humane, appropriate, and alterable. The family's connection to society is open and hopeful.

Sharp contrasts can be seen in troubled families: individual self-worth is low; communication becomes indirect, vague, dishonest. Family rules are rigid, nonnegotiable, and inhumane. The relationship to society is fearful, placating, and blaming.

Whatever a family's problem, says Satir, these key factors must be addressed to reduce pain and strengthen the family.[10]

When Froma Walsh appreciatively considered many models of the "normal" (that is, optimal, effective) family, including Satir's, she concluded that one needs to concentrate on processes, not on an invariant family form or set of traits. She identifies ten processes that, in interaction with each other, contribute to healthy family functioning. This is her eclectic, summary list:

1. Connectedness and commitment of members as a caring, mutually supportive relationship unit ("We are family").

2. Respect for individual differences, autonomy, and separate needs, fostering the development and well-being of members of each generation, from the youngest to the eldest.

3. For couples, a relationship characterized by mutual respect, support, and equitable sharing of power and responsibilities.

4. For nurturance, protection, and socialization of children and caretaking of other vulnerable family members, effective parental/executive leadership and authority.

5. Organizational stability, characterized by clarity, consistency, and predictability in patterns of interaction.

6. Adaptability: Flexibility to meet internal or external demands for change, to cope effectively with stress and problems that arise, and to master normative and nonnormative challenges and transitions across the life cycle.

7. Open communication characterized by clarity of rules and expectations, pleasurable interaction, and a range of emotional expression and empathic responsiveness.

8. Effective problem-solving and conflict-solution processes.

9. A shared belief system that enables mutual trust, problem mastery, connectedness with past and future generations, ethical values, and concern for the larger human community.

10. Adequate resources for basic economic security and psychosocial support in extended kin and friendship networks and from community and larger social systems.[11]

We can be grateful to the many social scientists who help us understand what covenant family living includes, what blocks it, and how those blocks can be overcome.

Implications for Family Ministry

Pastoral Leadership in Family Enrichment

At the heart of family enrichment is a focus on prevention. Two general strategies are central to preventing family crises: (1) providing timely information and making sensitive referrals and (2) teaching families coping skills. We will explore both in turn.

Information and referral. Effective family ministers know that they cannot and do not have to "do it all alone." They have taken the time to educate themselves about community resources. They know family therapists and counselors by their first names. They have up-to-date information on crisis centers, domestic abuse hotlines, and self-help groups. They know where to look when they need to help a family find highly specialized resources. They are glad to work with ecumenical colleagues and community partners to create new services when the need arises.

Vulnerability is the human condition. Yet it is not "culturally correct" to acknowledge the reality that we suffer and that we sometimes need help to be relational partners and family members. Congregations can be places where vulnerability is accepted, places that affirm "reaching out for help." Our faith has a great gift to offer families: reminding folks that God's presence in our lives is most powerfully experienced through our struggles and needs. Our pastoral leaders can render a great service: encouraging people to seek help with family issues before they become crises. Screening and legitimating community helping resources is crucial to supporting families effectively.

Teaching skills. Equal in importance to providing sound information and making appropriate referrals is teaching families the skills they need to cope with normal developmental issues and the occasional "unscheduled" crisis. Teaching skills in negotiation, communication, and conflict management is increasingly important as churches seek to minister with the diversity of contemporary families. Our focus in this section is on the whole intergenerational family system. So below we will look at intergenerational learning, family retreats and camps, parenting, and at family-supportive ministries with youth and through day-care programs.

The principle of life-long learning needs to inform the congregation's entire educational ministry. Learning does not end with adolescence. In fact adult learning may be the most transformative in one's lifetime.[12] Because people differ in their learning styles and preferences, many settings and a variety of classes, discipleship groups, workshops, and skill-learning experiences are required to meet a congregation's needs. Obviously the needs of older youth and young adults are different from the needs of young couples, first-time parents, older couples facing retirement, and so on.

Ecumenical cooperation in the educational task can multiply enormously the resources offered to members of one congregation. Capitalize on the power of well-planned retreats and mission or study trips to promote transformation in people and family systems.

Intergenerational Strategies

Most church education is peer based. It sends family members in different directions during church time, reinforcing the ageist patterns of our educational system and culture. As a result, generations do not understand one another and often can hardly speak the same language. In the

early 1970s Margaret Sawin invented an educational approach called
"family clusters" that moves in exactly the opposite direction.13

Family clusters are gatherings of four to six complete household
units of many kinds for common learning, celebrating, recreating, and
sharing. A cluster might include a single-parent family, an older couple,
a single young adult, and two or three two-parent families. The genius of
this approach is that it takes the family system as the learner. In family
clusters whole families are present, growing in their understanding of
their agenda, their rules, their goals, their conflicts. In family clusters
whole families learn skills in communication, problem solving, and conflict resolution that equip them to work on their family agenda with greater competence and success. Clusters can focus on the needs of specific
kinds of families, for example helping single-parent families identify
their strengths and support systems or helping blended families consider
what values, rituals, and practices they want to preserve from the units
composing their new family systems.

Family cluster leaders need knowledge of family systems thinking
and skills in group dynamics. They need skill in designing action-reflec-
tion experiences. The heart of family learning is to do something together
(share an experience) and then draw discoveries from it (reflect on their
common experience). Many congregations include teachers, mental
health workers, and adult educators and trainers with the skills needed
for cluster leadership. These people can also train others to lead clusters.
Leaders need to be well grounded in Scripture and have a mature understanding of the Christian faith. A leader team-approach is a must. Presbyterian Mariners (a couples and families program of the Presbyterian
Church USA) have developed several resources that lend themselves to
family clusters.14

Family Camps and Retreats

Here's the chief advantage of family camp and retreat settings: For a
day or a week you can "set the rules" for just about all aspects of life.
This means that participating family systems can experience helpful
patterns of communication, conflict resolution, or decision making for
several days with minimal distractions. You can hardly create a more
powerful learning community in which to introduce and internalize new

insights, skills, and attitudes! Theological principles can be applied in the group's life. People and families can get more than just a taste of what life could be like using, for example, respectful and esteem-building communication patterns. Camps and retreats can provide an "alternate culture" in which families can discover their Christian identity and function together in new, healthy ways.

Many resources designed for intergenerational groups can be used in camp and retreat settings. We've mentioned the materials from Presbyterian Mariners. Intergenerational resources from the Parenting for Peace and Justice Network lend themselves nicely to use in retreat or camp settings. Camps themselves may offer unique outdoor resources to use with families. For example, if a camp offers a ropes course, you might be able to use it as a "family problem solving" exercise, providing families an experience in cooperation.

The camp or retreat setting offers additional learning opportunities. You might give families a task, such as planning a hike for the whole group, planning a devotional time, or organizing a meal. The key learning element is providing a family reflection time after such activities. In recalling, analyzing, and generalizing from their experience in a common task, families learn better ways of communicating, making decisions, and resolving conflicts. By all means, encourage the use and exchange of musical, dramatic, and dance skills. Let families have the joy of teaching others what they enjoy and do well. Make use of cooperative intergenerational games (see the resources list), which are fun for all ages and teach noncompetitive ways of interacting. Games are a wonderful resource for most anything, from energizing a group to learning names to providing an experience on which older children and adults can reflect and learn.

Parenting

As a result of the trend toward smaller families, most of us grow up with hardly any experience of caring for younger children. Many of us have had little sustained exposure to infants and toddlers. We enter parenthood with few concrete ideas of what we are getting ourselves into! Some of us babysat when we were adolescents, but that is not adequate preparation for the day-by-day stress of meeting the needs of a demanding newborn or an energetic toddler. Few of us have a large repertoire of skills for parenting.

Some schools have responded by offering classes in family life education. Some clever teachers have asked individual students or teams of two to simulate caring for a baby for a week or two; the "baby" is a raw egg or sack of sugar. The rules are strict: The students may never leave their egg or sack unattended. They must dress it, "feed" it, and clean it on a schedule. They must make sure the "baby" is safe at all times. Such an exercise opens the eyes of young people about the realities of parenting. A church-based youth group could make use of this exercise to teach similar lessons.

Congregations that sponsor, house, or run a day-care or nursery school program have a wonderful opportunity to reach out to parents. Nursery school teachers often know a great deal about communicating with young children, have creative ideas about discipline, and are skilled in planning ways to keep preschoolers occupied in productive ways. Many parents need these skills. Seek to promote workshops, classes, and at least informal interactions between parents and day-care or nursery workers. Perhaps the center or school would be willing to sponsor and organize a series of parent education classes.

The nursery school related to Joe's church created a family forum program that offers parents classes in child development, skill-training workshops, forums, and book studies. A typical offering for a season might include a class called Discipline: How to Stop Yelling at My Child; a workshop on using natural and logical consequences; a course for fathers in Systematic Training for Effective Parenting (shortened to four weeks from nine to accommodate schedules and male attention spans); a class on adolescent girls; a book study on *Raising a Thinking Child;* forums on parenting issues in the nineties; and classes on kindergarten readiness. Parent education is an excellent way to reach out to your community with the message that your congregation is family friendly. Parent education classes and workshops are also good candidates for ecumenical sponsorship and participation.

You might also study a book on parenting in an adult church-school class. Numerous books on parenting are available from denominational sources and independent publishers. A few are listed in the resource list.

Youth Ministry

The Search Institute findings discussed above point toward what they
call "reinventing youth ministry"—developing a new form of program-
ming for high schoolers. A key, they believe, is recruiting trustworthy
adults who will give generously of themselves to young people. Unfortu-
nately their research shows that this is a relatively rare experience for
youth; only about a third are connected with nonparental adults. Youth
ministry that connects young people with caring and trustworthy adults,
teaches communication and relationship-building skills, and engages
youth in service projects has the greatest impact on reducing at-risk behaviors and instilling positive values. It should be encouraging to church
leaders to know that in communities with the lowest rates of at-risk behaviors among youth, 70 percent of the youth attend religious services.
In those communities with the highest rates of at-risk behavior, only half
the young people attend.[15] Youth ministry does make a difference!

Youth ministry has long been seen in isolation as strictly a peer-
oriented ministry. From our family systems perspective, however, the
family in which the young person lives needs to be a major concern. We
urge youth ministry planning that includes parents in its concern and its
programs. Again, the Search Institute researchers point to the importance
of equipping parents of youth with parenting skills, especially in the
areas of control, giving support, and values formation.

If developing family-inclusive youth ministry is a new direction for
your congregation, you could start by inviting parents and youth to meet
for a session to talk about "the issues between us." Invite youth to meet
in private and talk about the problems they have with their parents but
rarely have opportunity to resolve. During the same time, ask parents to
meet in private and list the issues as they see them. Then bring the two
groups together. Ask youth (or a representative ten or so) to sit in a circle
surrounded by the adults and discuss "the issues we want to raise with
our parents." This should be done without naming who brought up what
during the earlier peer discussions. During this time youth only are to
talk; parents are to listen. Then reverse roles, reminding the adults they
are not to rebut what they heard the youth say, rather they are to discuss
"the issues we want to raise with young people."

After the two groups have finished, ask youth to comment on the
issues they heard raised by parents that connect with the issues they

identified; then ask the parents the same question. List the issues that both have an interest in. Then brainstorm strategies for working through them. Perhaps a retreat will be suggested on one of the topics raised; perhaps a series of parent-youth dialogues; perhaps a communications skill-building workshop. Could several family clusters deal with some of the issues raised? Consider video tapes that parents and/or youth might view in their groups/classes. Do you get some ideas for adult education classes from this exchange? A sermon series?

Close this time together by seeking an agreement about next steps. Perhaps the group will want to meet again and use the same format to clarify where parents and youth stand on one of the issues raised. In any event, you will be launched toward a family systems approach to youth ministry. For further help, see the new book *Life-Changing Events for Youth and their Families*.[16]

4. Strengthen Commitment to the Covenant of Marriage

A fourth dimension to a congregation's family ministry: Strengthen commitment to the covenant of marriage by seeking healthy marriages/partnerships.

For marriage to be successful, spouses need to have reasonable expectations and make reasonable efforts. In our society, there have been extremely high expectations—of an enriching, ongoing romance similar to the earliest days of dating. This is expected but with virtually no preparation for making it a reality. It takes much more preparation to obtain a driver's license (some) than to obtain a marriage license (none) or to parent a child (none).

There are some signs of the failure of high expectations for marriage: Some make the decision not to marry at all. The "practical" wisdom seems to be "Why spoil a good thing? Let's just stay lovers." In our opinion, too high expectations or too low expectations of marriage are both predictors of failure.

There need to be reasonable expectations and reasonable effort to fulfill those expectations. We love the answer that one of the advice columnists gave to a starry-eyed young couple asking to know how to make their love last forever. She responded, "It's simple. You work like a dog at it."

A deeply personally satisfying relationship in marriage deserves attention and energy. It deserves education and practice in human relations and negotiating skills, preparation for marriage, marriage enrichment opportunities, and more.

Effective Marriages

What makes for an effective marriage?

In effective marriages the differences between male and female expectations are acknowledged and negotiated. We hope that some of these differences will decrease in the current and coming generations. But there will always be some issues that need to be faced.

Deborah Tannen has served us well by exploring how differently men and women talk to people of their own gender and the opposite gender. Even the awareness that we only appear to be talking the same language can increase communication across language gaps! As a pastoral counselor, Dick has lent Tannen's book *You Just Don't Understand* to a number of couples. Without exception, it increased their awareness of times they were missing each other, and it sensitized each to the other's communication efforts.

An effective marriage is based in an approximate equality of power. No one is financially blackmailed. Financial resources are the right and responsibility of both and of each.

No one is sexually coerced in an effective marriage. (Sadly, the incidence of marital rape is reported to be distressingly high.) Equal partners make equal decisions about sex.

In an effective marriage one spouse is not overworked and another overleisured; rather, the workload is shared. Tasks are distributed through family negotiation, not dictated by cultural gender role patterns.

Couples in healthy marriages continually improve their skills for managing conflict and negotiating needs. Studies indicate that many marriages break up not for a lack of satisfaction in many areas, but from the inability to settle the conflicts in one or a few areas. Effective negotiating skills can be taught to people of goodwill. Wise couples and churches include this area in their repertoire.

Effective marriages keep romance alive. This also needs more attention and support than we might imagine. Sexual attraction as the basis for marriage and as a major factor in deciding whether to stay together is a relatively new phenomenon. (As we noted, across centuries and cultures, typically the family chose spouses, based on economic and family welfare considerations.) What's more, the church has not been very good at supporting satisfying sexual communion in marriage. We church folks have long talked about agape love—unconditional, nonsexual, not necessarily mutual love. We have neglected the Bible's message affirming sexual love. Who ever preaches on texts from the "Song of Songs"? How many of our congregants know that this erotic poem is part of the Bible? The power of sexual relations to reenergize a partnership and renew covenantal commitments needs to be lifted up and affirmed. The sustaining and comforting role of mutual pleasuring needs to be celebrated as the gift of God that it is. Let us not hesitate to reclaim the biblical roots that undergird the goodness of romance and sexual love.

Of course this aspect will change over the years of a marriage. Couples need to be ready for that, and churches may be able to give a gift to couples—skill in acknowledging, discussing, and rekindling romantic sexual love.

Effective marriages need to survive many transitions. Job changes, the possible birth of children, possible leaving of children, possible return of children, moves, health issues, aging parents, retirement, deaths—these are some of the occasions of change for the long-term couple. With each passage, a marriage changes in some important aspects.

One particular couple, married as teenagers, went through two eras of child bearing and many career and role changes. They have now been married nearly forty-five years. They describe these transitions in this way: "We marry, then dis-marry, then remarry"—having faced and negotiated the necessary transitions. Or as another man described his long-term marriage: "I've been married to five different women—they were all Abigail."

Couples that persist through crises, challenges, and changes may discover many rewards as they learn to accept aspects of each other and as they quit trying to reform the other. There may be a growth of comfort with each other, a sense of a richer, more complex relationship. Mutual memories may be a source of marital treasure. Such possibilities need to be discussed and celebrated in church marriage groups; the culture gives little credence or credit to the possibility of satisfying long-term relationships.

Some time ago, Jeannette and Robert Lauer did a study of "Marriages Made to Last." They surveyed and interviewed more than three hundred couples married for fifteen years or more who said their marriages were happy, successful, and enduring.

From thirty-nine statements they asked couples to select the ones that best showed why their marriages had lasted. Here are some of the top rated items:

- My spouse is my best friend . . .
- I like my spouse as a person . . .
- Marriage is a long-term commitment . . .
- Marriage is sacred . . .
- We agree on aims and goals . . .
- My spouse has grown more interesting . . .
- I want the relationship to succeed . . .
- An enduring marriage is important to social stability . . .
- We laugh together . . .[17]

The Lauers found two common themes among these happily married couples. (1) They really liked each other and exhibited qualities of caring, giving, integrity, and a sense of humor. (2) They shared a belief in marriage as a long-term commitment and sacred institution. These couples viewed marriage as a task that sometimes demands gritting one's teeth and plunging ahead in spite of difficulties. One woman told them, "I'll tell you why we stayed together. I am just too darn stubborn to give up."

The church has an opportunity for life-long marriage and family education, preparation for marriage, and marriage enrichment and counseling. It is a theological-ethical obligation that comes both from scriptural teachings and the urgent pressures of the age.

Implications for Family Ministry

Pastoral Roles

What can pastors and congregations do to strengthen committed partnerships? Research does not point the way as clearly as we might like. For
example, David and Vera Mace, the founders of the marriage enrichment
movement in North America, held that their research showed the futility
of premarital counseling. Because a couple prior to marriage is too "star-
ry eyed" to look at each other and the relationship realistically, the Maces
discouraged pastors from investing significantly in premarital counseling.

On the other hand, the Prepare-Enrich Inventory for use with couples contemplating marriage claims to predict with about 80 percent
accuracy whether partnerships are likely to succeed or fail. The inventory
provides valuable feedback about a relationship's areas of strength and
weaknesses. That 10 percent of couples taking the inventory decide to
postpone or cancel wedding plans suggests its power.[18]

Some churches insist on premarital preparation as a matter of principle. For example, the Catholic Church generally requires extensive
premarital preparation and produces materials to help pastors and couples. Certainly the high divorce rate motivates us to consider what can be
done premaritally to strengthen relationships. While we disagree with
those who see the clergy as all powerful in reducing divorce rates, we do
believe that clergy are accountable for helping each couple face the nature of the decision they are making. In our opinion strategies to build
and sustain committed relationships need to address both premarital and
marital issues.

Dick likes to maintain the special relationship he has with couples
whose weddings he performs. He invites them back after three months,
six months, and a year for a check-up. This is a time to rejoice together
in the fulfillment that committed partnership brings. It is also a time to
identify issues that have arisen and need attention, before they become
big problems. A tickler file in the desk or computer or a note on the
calendar can help the harried pastor recall that lovely couple that would
be pleased to get a "three-month note" from their pastor reminding them
that their relationship deserves celebration!

Strengthening marital partnerships should be a congregational priority. This can happen as clergy interpret to the congregation what is happening to marriages today, just how destructive the cultural milieu is, and how difficult economic stresses are for many couples. Some older members may be troubled by the ways their children and grandchildren are going about courtship, especially if this involves cohabitation. Theological interpretation from the pulpit—what a committed partnership is—can be instructive. Giving clear messages about the unacceptability of violence and the importance of shared and equal power in intimate relationships can help congregations recognize the possibility that the church has something credible to say about partnerships.

Clergy have a wide repertoire of strategies for strengthening marriages. These include group approaches; the use of "wise couples" to work with others, couple to couple; testing instruments; and counseling approaches.

Enrichment Opportunities

Many couples benefit from structured marriage enrichment retreats. The Maces' research, mentioned above, identifies critical times when marriage enrichment experiences can make a major contribution.[19] These are after the first six months to a year; after about ten years; and when the family nest empties and the couple has more time and opportunity to focus on their relationship. Marriage enrichment is not therapy, and it is not recommended for a couple in trouble. It is a way healthy couples can make their relationships better. Information about marriage enrichment programs and leaders is available from ACME, the Association of Couples for Marriage Enrichment (see organizations listed in the resource list). ACME was founded by David and Vera Mace to promote healthy and growing marriages. Another movement that claims success in strengthening marriages is Marriage Encounter (see resources). This movement is lay led and has "expressions" in many faith traditions.

Support Groups

Enrichment weekends or encounters are not every couple's cup of tea. Some couples find support in a less intense dinner-discussion group format. Taking turns hosting a potluck or cooperative meal, discussing is-sues, such as marriage, parenting, and social change, builds connections among couples and surfaces resources for strengthening their partnerships.

You might try couple-based discipleship groups. These groups covenant to share personally, study Scripture, pray, and recreate together. Discipleship groups represent a significant way to enrich committed partnerships and connect them explicitly to the resources and tradition of Christian faith.

Building Skills

Another important way to enrich intimate partnerships is by building communication skills. Giving couples opportunities to learn better patterns of communication can prevent some relational stress and equip couples to reduce other stresses. Skills in self-disclosure, active listening, problem solving, and negotiating are important, but don't neglect a key element—helping couples maintain and enhance the esteem of both self and partner. Skilled communication can be more than a way to increase the chances of relational survival; it can be a way to build the strength of the relationship. A research-based program called Couple Communication has proven highly successful (see resources). The organization provides training to use its materials as well as a roster of certified instructors.

Couple-to-Couple Interventions

From time to time pastors are confronted with couples in trouble. In such cases couple-to-couple intervention is gaining recognition. Recently a few congregations have discovered that mature couples having experienced the vicissitudes of conflict and reconciliation in their own marriages can play a critical role in helping other couples facing difficulties.[20] This approach builds on the insight of many marriage enrichment leaders—that couple leadership is critical to effective enrichment retreats. The credibility and practical experience of mature partners is a unique gift.

5. Develop a Theology and Strategy for Ministry with Singles

In the previous chapter we noted that in the New Testament singleness is affirmed, praised, and lived. This was a new step and is also in contrast to the second-class status too often given to single people by congregations. Single people are not outside the scope of family ministries! Because one lives alone or has not married or is divorced or widowed does not mean one is without family. The concept of family systems tells us that all of us are connected with family relationships and rarely only in memory.

Much of what has been said already about family support applies to single people in our congregations. They need to be included in family clusters, family retreats, and all church events. Poor indeed is the church where coming without a partner bars one from participation and leadership!

The new reality is that while more than 90 percent of adults marry at least once in a lifetime, at any moment nearly 50 percent of adults are currently single. It is estimated that by the year 2000, singleness will be the status of the majority of adults. They have many and diverse gifts and needs arising out of a variety of life situations. "Singleness" includes adults of any age who are never married, divorced, or widowed—with or without children.

This reality impacts all congregations. It calls congregations to develop sensitivity and support toward a new—close at hand—mission field. The majority of adults is a worthy population on which to focus! Many in this population are quite aware that the church has had a bias in favor of married people with children. A burden of proof will lie with the congregation to demonstrate that it really cares for people who are single.

A Theology of Singleness

The first step toward ministry is a consciousness-altering theology of singleness. As we pointed out, our Bible leads the way to such a theology. We are told, for example, of numerous people who served God greatly and who were single all or part of their lives. Ruth, Elijah, Jeremiah, Daniel, Jesus, and Paul were among these. Several of these faithful leaders, especially Jesus and Paul, spoke of singleness as a gift out of their commitment to God's reign.

The Bible affirms that each person is created by God in the image of God, without regard to marital status. While the Bible does say that it is not good for people to be alone, that is not a blanket endorsement of marriage; it is an awareness that each of us lives in relationship with many people.

The Bible tells of God's unconditional love for each person and of God's spiritual gifts to each person individually. Each individual person can experience God's creation, image, unconditional love, salvation, giftedness, and mission—and this is by no means an exhaustive list.[21] Starting from such a theology of singleness, each congregation will need to develop a strategy of ministry with single adults.

Issues in Singles' Ministry

Ministry to singles must start with respectful and attentive open-ended listening to singles within their present community. Such conversation will likely raise a basic question: Should singles' ministry be one of integration and inclusion or a special outreach to a distinct group? Which approach a congregation takes depends on a number of factors: How large is the single population in the congregation? At which ages are single people concentrated? How open are programs in the church to their participation and how relevant to the issues single people raise? In many congregations there may well be room for both approaches. In some congregations young adult groups mixing married people and singles have been known to work well. Discipleship groups can easily minister to both coupled and single people.

Most congregations, however, can and should provide opportunities for single people to meet together, reflect on their experiences, and enjoy one another. Retreats, trips, and projects are a way for even the smallest group to have a good experience together. Ecumenical cooperation in singles' ministries may make the most sense in many communities. On the other hand, congregations with large populations of single adults may well be called to offer their community a singles' ministry, through organized church school classes, fellowship groups, and sports and social events.

Implications for Ministry

Lifting Up the Presence and Gifts of Single Adults

Single people need to be visible in the leadership, congregational life, and worship of the church. All the roles of leadership should be open to single people. Congregations need their talents, whether as musicians, educators, artists, administrators, preachers, dramatists, or quiet thinkers. Sometimes the strongest advocates for children and families are single people. Margaret Sawin, the originator of the family cluster model, was a life-long single person. She never forgot that she was "family" too!

Inclusive Opportunities

Opportunities for single adults to meet children, connect with other family units, and share deeply with all others in the congregation are important. Being part of a family cluster is one powerful way for single people to work on their own family-of-origin issues as well as bond with children and parents in other family units. It also is a way their gifts can be shared with other family units of the congregation. Similarly, "family" retreats and camping experiences need to be inclusive of single adults who may feel the need to connect with the "extended family" of the congregation. Young people need to know that being a twosome is not the only way to live a fulfilled life.

Sometimes single people are able to give more of themselves to the church because they do not have other family members in their care. Congregations need to beware of exploiting single people or simply assuming that they are more available than coupled members of the community. When a single person makes an extraordinary gift of self to a congregation, that gift should be affirmed and recognized for the grace it truly is.

When congregations offer communication-skills training, retreats focused on significant relationships, or courses on how to discipline children with love and firmness, be sure that single members are welcomed. They need skills in communication as much as coupled members. They have significant relationships in their lives. They care about how children are treated.

Focused Opportunities

Certainly there is a place for single people to work on their common
experiences. As a group that is sometimes marginalized in our culture,
single people for whatever reason may sometimes feel they all share
some common oppressions! Single groups may be segmented by life
experience or interests. People who have never married may be faced
with different issues than single parents, who may want to discuss issues
different from those facing widowed people.

Networks of single people who share the same experience of singleness are important. Older single women in a congregation Joe served
developed a telephone care network. They organized a phone tree and
checked up on each other every morning. If someone didn't answer the
call, a pastor or other helper was dispatched to check up on the unrespon-
sive member.

Single parents, especially early in their experience, profit from talking with others experiencing similar challenges. Hosting a Parents without Partners group is one way to serve single parents in the congregation
and reach out to the community at the same time.

Where single people are clustered in the young adult years, a group
for study, recreation, and socializing is an important ministry. Congregations have found that starting a church school class for young single
adults often works well. Opportunities for socializing and recreating can
be added. It doesn't take a large group to start a class, and it may be the
start of something big!

In your repertoire also consider retreats, camping trips, and national
conferences for single adults. Unless the church responds with openness
and welcome, single adults will organize their lives without it. A comprehensive resource on singles ministry is outlined in *Single in the Church*
by Kay Collier-Slone.[22]

Summary

In this chapter we've identified five basic dimensions of family ministry.
Within a framework of family support, we've offered suggestions for
how to implement ministries that create a family-friendly culture in
church and community. We explored the importance of a family's sense

of mission and becoming an enriching community. We lifted up strategies for strengthening marital partnerships and tried to outline a theology of singleness.

In the next chapter we will confront seven challenges for family ministry and offer strategies for meeting them.

CHAPTER 5

Challenges for Family Ministry

The family remains the locus of the deepest and most resonant ties, the most enduring hopes, the most intractable conflicts, the most poignant tragedies, and the sweetest triumphs human life affords to the vast majority of us. Passion, intimacy, and the surprising depth of love and hate, and the astonishing strength of human endurance and concern—families evoke all of these.

—Jean Bethke Elshtain[1]

From our discussion of five basic dimensions of congregational family ministry, we turn to seven challenges that face leaders seeking to minister to contemporary families. These challenges call, first, for ethical discernment, and then for a bold response by the Christian church. They also call for innovative approaches to ministry.

Three Preliminary Comments

Commending Support Circles

In chapter 4 we indicated that family support is a key concept in our proposed new paradigm for family ministry. Within that framework we commend a general strategy—the support circle.

A support circle is a group of people who covenant to stand with an individual or family who has major need. Let's say an elderly person nearing the end of life requires much care. A support circle can help family caregivers by providing respite, offering financial counsel, giving emotional support, and being a sounding board and collaborator for decision making. Or when a family is caring for a member with chronic disease or disability, a circle can be the life line for the family, preventing institutionalization. In many communities support circles help families with a developmentally disabled youth or adult plan for and organize a life that includes work, friendships, and recreation. A support circle can be there for such an individual when family members are no longer able to provide support. The concept can be applied to many families in many circumstances.

A variation on the concept is family-to-family support circles. What a difference it makes when a single parent is linked with another family to be there emotionally, to help with practical chores, to be an extended family for celebrations, holidays, and to offer support in hard times! Think what it would mean to a family with a teenager acting out or battling addiction or anorexia to have the support of caring friends who will help share the struggle and offer practical help.

Support circles are a way to strengthen families that have no out-of-the-ordinary agenda other than the typical challenges of trying to raise children in the midst of economic stress, surrounded by media obsessed with violence and exploitative sexuality. The Parenting for Peace and Justice Network has developed a related concept of family support groups to enrich families spiritually and emotionally. These groups consist of several family units of all kinds; they're intergenerational family circles that gather for meals, fun, worship, holidays, mission projects, and study. Such family support groups give isolated seniors the opportunity to grandparent youngsters. They provide single adults a place for connecting with a family of choice. They transform parenting from a lonely struggle to an experience of solidarity and security.

Acknowledging the Power of Ritual

The second preliminary comment we want to make is about the power of ritual in the Christian community. One unique way Christian congregations support families is by ritualizing important moments. Congregations can and should *invent* rituals that respond to contemporary families. Rituals are a powerful means of reinforcing commitments, healing wounds, and celebrating acts of courage and times of passage. Churches traditionally recognize important transitions in a family's life. We are familiar with weddings, baptisms or dedications of children, and funerals or memorial services. These traditional forms, however, do not easily accommodate remarriage and blended family formation. Nor do they directly and sensitively address divorce, same sex partnerships, nonmarital cohabitation, adoption, or unwed parenthood.

Some will argue that these latter experiences are to be avoided and should not be marked with church ceremony. It is not uncommon to hear the champions of two-parent families call for "restigmatizing" divorce, as if that would help marriages to endure. Our response is different. We believe that stigmatizing tragic decisions is sub-Christian. Instead, we know that offering blessing can promote healing, integrity, and spiritual health. So, for example, we urge that religious communities need to gather around the divorcing member or member couple and offer a public and spiritual occasion for redefining their relationship.

Further, we believe that for some cohabiting couples a ritual that recognizes their relationship as being "serious" will strengthen their commitment and bring it into the congregation's care. Celebrating an adoption, a sensitive ceremony acknowledging the birth of a child to an unzwed parent, ritually recognizing what is happening when a blended family comes together—all seem to be ways by which the riches of the Christian faith can be brought to bear on circumstances that cry out for supportive congregational action. It's a social fact that lesbian and gay couples establish enduring partnerships as stable and long lived as many marriages. What is most congruent with Gospel values—to ignore such life-giving, faithful commitments or to offer recognition, blessing, and the support of the wider Christian family? Congregations ready to reach out and welcome gay and lesbian Christians will need to consider how they can recognize and honor with appropriate ritual the partnership commitments these believers will make.

Matching Congregational Gifts with Needs

Our third preliminary comment is that we do *not* envision *all* congregations responding to *all* the challenges we identify in this chapter. Rather, we counsel a process of matching a congregation's gifts to the needs of its families, undergirded by a strong faith that God does not call any of us to do everything! A church's call to ministry is to be heard in the context of correlating needs with available gifts. No one congregation is the whole church, and ecumenical ministries—for example, with blended families—may be the most faithful. On the other hand, a particular congregation's ministry with divorced people may serve the whole community. Another congregation may discover that it is called to be the one that reaches out to gay and lesbian folk. We are confident that God's call will be heard, and in that confidence we offer these suggestions for ministry in seven challenge areas.

1. Ministry and the Challenge of Divorce

We have reported the changed legal climate for divorce; the huge annual numbers of divorce (virtually every family is touched in some way); the wide variety of Bible passages that speak of divorce; and an interpretation we feel is faithful to these Bible teachings.

We suggested that Jesus' teachings about divorce not be made into a new law. Rather, these teachings are an ethical ideal and an affirmation that God is at work knitting relationships, weaving partnerships, and offering to bless them. Our question now is how to be faithful practitioners of what we heard these Bible passages saying. Part of our faithfulness is to make every effort to help marriages be meaningful, enriching, and lasting. Another part is to recognize that divorces do occur; sometimes they need to occur. Jesus said that Moses allowed divorce "for the hardness of our hearts." Relationships do harden, become brittle, destructive, and abusive. Divorce may be better than continued destructiveness within the family.

So churches need to develop the paired strategies of (1) doing everything possible to strengthen and honor marriage and (2) having a system in place that offers multifaceted support and acceptance to every person in divorcing families. And we need to uphold both aspects being confident that they are not contradictory. Divorced people must not be seen as second-class citizens.

The Cost of Divorce

No one is happy over the high divorce rates. The pain and suffering in this situation may be even greater than is commonly recognized. Don and Carol Browning cite a study that one in five children under eighteen "has a learning, emotional, behavioral or developmental problem that can be traced to the dissolution of the two-parent family." This grows to one in four teenagers, and one in three male teenagers.[2] One might ask what is cause and what is effect? Emotional, behavioral, and developmental problems are hard on marriages.

Ways to Reduce the Pain

In response to the Brownings' contentions, Betty Vos points out that these dire consequences are not automatic and that the impact is not as large as their statistics indicate. Vos says four factors can decrease the negative effect (and increase the positive effect) of divorce from troubled relationships.

Finances. Two households are more expensive than one, and usually women and children suffer financially from divorce more than do men—for two reasons: Most court-mandated child-support arrangements fall short of the children's actual needs, and less than half of all divorced fathers meet even these minimal obligations. This issue cries out for attention. Vos reports, "Economic status alone accounts for a major portion of the adjustment problems that children of divorce experience."[3]

Family conflict, during the marriage, throughout the divorce process, and after the divorce decree. Prolonged intense conflict between the parents hurts everyone, including children, whether there is divorce or not. Such conflict may impair children's development as they are preoccupied by fears and anxieties stirred by these battles. The children may be caught up in custody battles, child-support fights, and spying tasks.

Continued involvement of both parents in their children's lives. If the parents can get beyond severe conflict, the children will fare better when both parents participate actively in their lives. (Studies also show that fathers who see their children regularly do better at keeping up on child-support payments.) The need for other-parent involvement applies equally to mother-headed homes (currently 90 percent) and father-headed homes (approximately 10 percent).

A support network. At a most vulnerable time, divorcing adults need to feel loved, understood, accepted, and supported. Both partners need this. Some can accept such support in groups. Others may accept it only one on one. The lack of such an adult support network may lead divorced parents to seek primary emotional support from their children, unintentionally overburdening their children in yet another way. Children also need support—someone who will listen to their fears and problems, someone who will assure them that the divorce is not their fault.

Divorce and the Church

The church has many ministering opportunities with the divorcing and divorced family. One opportunity involves spiritual welcome, acceptance, and support. Tim Emerick-Cayton notes, "In spite of our faith in God's everlasting love, many divorcing couples experience condemnation—both internally and by the community of faith. This condemnation often leads to a downward spiritual spiral."[4] The congregation will need to be especially welcoming, supportive, and affirming to people who may be all too ready to blame themselves, unstable at times, quite angry at times. Church folks can realize there is no "quick fix" from the pain of divorce. It will take years.

On the other hand, a woman told Dick, "My divorce was a spiritual experience. Somehow I was able to claim the promises of God to help, sustain, comfort, and forgive. I did have to leave one church and find another. In this whole process I was able to hold on to what my faith promised me."

Divorcing people often drop out of church. Shame, avoidance of past associations, the judgmental attitude of congregations, and the perception that the congregation is no place to look for support lead many divorcing people to disappear. We feel congregations need to look at themselves and seek to communicate a new message to the divorcing or divorced.

It is perhaps unrealistic to expect that, when a couple in the congregation divorces, both partners will continue in the church. That scenario may simply be too painful. The couple may decide that one of them "gets the church." Their decision needs to be respected. Attention should be paid to how the departing member is let go. Appropriate closure has healing potential. We will proffer some suggestions about ritual below.

Implications for Ministry

Before the Decision to End a Relationship

The first strategy we want to suggest is the clearness meeting, described in chapter 4. A couple contemplating separation or divorce might choose to sit with some trusted friends and seek greater clarity about their decision. The friends will help by asking open-ended questions and praying for God's guidance on behalf of the couple.

In Joe's church a couple deciding to separate for a time told the congregation and asked for prayer and support during their time apart. Their gesture did much to empower their friends to reach out and be of real help. Their openness freed others from the fear of confronting the reality of a strained relationship. After some months apart, this couple came together again, and their announcement of their decision was an occasion of much jubilation!

During Separation and Divorce

A second strategy to help the former partners is to offer a support circle for each: a few friends who will not take sides but will listen and offer emotional and practical support. A former wife may be needing help to find work or restart a career. A support circle can be the beginning of a network. Children may need care as well as emotional support. A support circle can be a resource to them.

Support for Children Whose Parents Are Divorced

A third strategy focuses on children. Children of divorcing or divorced parents often blame themselves for the end of their parents' marriage. All kinds of regressive behavior show up (such as bed-wetting and trouble going to sleep) and sometimes problems develop at school. Adolescents whose parents divorce are at risk for depression. Groups in which children can share their feelings and perceptions, guided by a skilled facilitator, can help them survive the divorce and minimize the trauma. This strategy may need to be pursued ecumenically or in partnership with a community mental health or family counseling agency. Its benefits cannot be overestimated.

Mediation

Supportive friends within a church may be able to help divorcing people avoid costly adversarial court fights. They can point the way to more reasonable mediation techniques, those available from the court and from the private sector. Mediation is "the use of a neutral third party to assist divorcing couples and families in reaching mutual agreement on all divorce-related issues."[5] It is often possible to preserve values undermined by the adversarial process. Tim Emerick-Cayton, a divorce mediator, describes this as a "ministry of reconciliation," by which he means coming to terms with the divorce itself, learning to show respect for one's divorcing spouse, and reaching agreement on practical matters.

It is important that church members be educated about mediation as an alternative to adversarial divorce proceedings. Even if there are no divorcing couples in the church when the information is presented, many members will have extended family members or friends who can benefit from this alternative. Any congregation can provide brochures or other easy-to-pick-up information about mediation services in the local area.

Rituals

A few congregations are experimenting with divorce rituals (see the resource list) to bring dignity and closure to a marital relationship. Divorce is a major life crisis; for healing to begin, the death of what was needs to be recognized. The good that was needs to be affirmed and the loss needs to be mourned. Why should the Christian community be content to leave this process to therapists when the most powerful resources for healing and resurrection are spiritual?

A divorce ritual can put in place a new covenant between the parties that defines what their future relationship will be. This raises property settlements and custody agreements to an appropriate level of solemnity. What was done in the wedding before God and the community of faith needs to be undone and redone in the presence of God and the community. Ritualizing a divorce affords the couple an opportunity to seek pardon for what has been broken and receive the assurance of the faith community that God forgives and renews us even when we fail badly. It also gives the community a way to be supportive of both partners.

Often only one partner is church-related or feels the need to ritualize the ending of a marriage.

At Joe's church in a healing service the hurt and brokenness experienced by a divorcing person is acknowledged. The need to make this painful decision is publicly recognized and the prayers of the community for healing are lifted. The death of a relationship is mourned and the hope of resurrection to new life is affirmed. Usually healing services in this congregation include an anointing with oil, a traditional way the Christian community ministers to those in deep pain.

Not talking in community about great crises, great pain, and great failure is never healthy for the human spirit. ("Family secrets" are grist for the family therapist's mill.) Ritual is one way to dispel the secret, bring light to a troubling experience, and proclaim the Christian hope at just the moment when a pilgrim needs to hear and believe it.

2. Ministry and the Challenge of Remarriage

Emily and John Visher, who have given such sensitive attention to remarried families for many years, predict that by the year 2000, remarried families will outnumber all other kinds of American families. They suggest, "No longer is a step family an 'alternative' family; it is a normative family with its own challenges and rewards."[6] Churches and families that want to strengthen covenantal relationships will need to overcome negative misconceptions and develop sensitivities and skills in supporting this family type.

A number of negative stereotypes need to be overcome. The terms *stepmother, stepfather,* and *stepchild* can be used to imply something less than satisfactory. Sadly, some therapists and educators may share these pessimistic views of this family type.

Tasks of Remarriage Families

It is more accurate to say that folks moving into this family type face a formidable number of issues and tasks if they are to form a deep community with each other. The Vishers summarize stepfamily characteristics and tasks in the following table:

Stepfamily Characteristics	Stepfamily Tasks
1. Begins after many losses and changes	1. Dealing with losses and changes
2. Incongruent individual, marital, family life cycles	2. Negotiating different developmental needs
3. Children and adults all come with expectations from previous families	3. Establishing new traditions
4. Parent-child relationships predate the new couple	4. Developing a solid couple bond and forming new relationships
5. Biological parent elsewhere in actuality or in memory	5. Creating a "Parenting Coalition"
6. Children often members of two households	6. Accepting continual shifts in household composition
7. Legal relationships between step-parent and children is societal or non-existent	7. Risking involvement despite little ambiguous support[7]

With these many adjustments, one might expect the early days of a new remarried family to be filled with confusion and anxiety. A teenager living in a stepfamily told the Vishers, "Everybody goes through trauma and everybody survives. At the beginning I thought I wouldn't get through. Now I think I'm stronger for it."[8]

At the same time, a successful remarriage family has many gifts to offer both the adults and the children within the family.

> A successful [remarriage] family . . . provides exposure to a variety of lifestyles, opinions, feelings, and enriching relationships. . . . The previously divorced adult, wiser from hindsight, forms a new type of marital relationship with the opportunity to parent and to benefit from a supportive suprasystem. In [remarriage], children can learn to appreciate and respect differences in people and ways of living, can receive affection and support from a new stepparent and the new suprasystem, and can observe the remarried parent in a good and loving marital relationship, using this as a model for their own future love relationship. If an only child, he or she may gain the experience of cooperation that a subsystem with other children offers.[9]

From our vantage point, we see that many remarried couples have made a much better choice the second time around. They are some of the most stable and creative families in our congregations.

Implications for Ministry

Pastoral Roles

All of those benefits can come in remarried families, but nothing is automatic. This family type is often quite fragile, especially in its early years. Pastors who want to be covenant-faithful with people contemplating formation of a remarried family will want to (1) help them be sure they have healed from the pain of earlier relationships before entering a new one; (2) provide specialized premarriage and early marriage counsel; and (3) find ways to offer ongoing support.

How friendly are congregations to families with complex histories and webs of relationships? By the turn of the millennium will these families be in church? If so, how willing will they be to be noticed as "different"? We think there is an interesting collusion that goes on between congregations and blended families. The congregation is glad they are there so long as they "fit in" with all the "regular" families. The blended family, perhaps somewhat tired of having to explain itself at school, at work, and in the neighborhood, is happy to be invisible.

The ambivalence of blended families about facing their special needs requires pastors to strike a balance between a focus on blended families and integrating them into "regular" family activities of the congregation. We agree with the Vishers that blended families do have some tasks they need to face if they are to become all that they wish for and can be. Certainly many of these tasks are basic to any family system, but blended families have to undo and redo earlier work on these tasks. Classes, workshops, retreats, or other experiences that help all families will be appreciated by the blended family.

Whole-Family Strategies

The family cluster model lends itself to working with blended families. In that intergenerational setting, the whole family can deal with many of the issues they face. For example, blended families need to take account of their multiple heritages. Heritage can include everything from putting the lid back on the jelly jar after spreading the toast to how Christmas is to be celebrated or birthdays observed.

Families have sacred cows, little habits or practices that are unquestioned but generate a lot of heat when violated! In a blended family, these need to be acknowledged and the varying expectations of family members must be accommodated and negotiated. Traditions, religious observances, stories of forebears, all need to be reworked and used by the family to enrich and ground itself. Ignoring these simply lays the groundwork for conflict and unhappiness. In a cluster with three or four other families facing the same issues, this can be done in an affirming spirit of fun.

A family cluster could also help a blended family make rules explicit. Discipline will be more palatable and effective if the whole family has agreed on some ground rules. If they can learn a process to negotiate and renegotiate agreements, they will have powerful skills to help them resist the centrifugal forces pulling them apart.

Other topics to consider for a cluster of blended families include church relationship and faith, the handling of money, sexuality (especially important to a blended family with older children or adolescents), and simply acknowledging and even celebrating the complex family system that is theirs! Children in a blended family can come to recognize that many adults love them and are there to care for them. Working with the blended family in the context of others like them can lead to such a positive and happy outcome.

Support Groups

Both of us have had some experience trying to reach out to remarried couples. We have found fear and resistance to facing and working through the issues that come with blending two families. Couples are often reluctant to explore what being remarried means for good reason: They have experienced the death of at least one previous relationship and understandably are afraid that, if they turn over a rock in their current relationship, all kinds of bad things will crawl out. In Dick's experience, it is often necessary to work ecumenically and in interfaith settings to create a viable support group for remarried couples. It is worth the effort because a group in which positive things are happening will draw others. In many communities a couple may feel "safer" attending a support group outside their congregation. Then they are freer to participate with "regular" couples in their own congregations. This meets their preference not to be set apart in congregational life.

If Your Congregation Has a Large Singles' Group

In many communities a particular congregation has "the singles' group," which may be fed from many churches. These congregations have learned that the singles' group produces many remarriages. If you are such a church, consider ongoing remarried couples' groups to support the new marriages coming out of the singles' program.

Rituals

Divorced people who remarry, especially where there are children, must renegotiate the relationship with previous spouses. It will happen, either intentionally and openly or covertly, and in the latter case probably accompanied by stressful emotions and relational fallout. Formalizing that renegotiation with a new covenant that expresses expectations, identifies boundaries, and reaffirms commitment to any children involved can, we believe, facilitate formation of the new family. Especially when older children or youth are part of the new blended family, ritual can offer a sense of normality, safety, and continuity that will help children feel more secure. There are few models available. But the essence of it is to make explicit the promises each person is making to the others in the new extended network of family relationships. (Write the Commission on Family Ministries listed in the resources for recovenanting ceremonies.)

3. Ministry and the Challenge of Two-Career Families

This is a topic on which there is great ambivalence. For example, in his analysis of the future of the American family, George Barna writes,

> The "second shift" that women work at home after spending time at a job is wearing down millions of women. Reports of illnesses, acute fatigue, emotional exhaustion, depression, and unfulfilled expectations suggest that many women are not satisfied with their existence. Even the forms of assistance designed to make the "super moms" possible, such as child-care centers, have failed to provide the kind of help that women need.[10]

Barna points out that in 1991 a nationwide Roper survey of women discovered that for the first time in a number of years, women's top lifestyle preference was no longer career plus family. Many continue to work outside the home for a number of reasons, one of the most basic being harsh economic realities, to which we referred in chapter 1.

Having acknowledged economic need, many find that a fitting, manageable two-career plan for their family provides stimulus for growth and contribution by both parents.

Both congregations and individual family units may have ambivalence over this pattern. There may be such strong and mixed feelings that discussion is strained or impossible. Many aspects of this topic need much more discussion, rather than sweeping generalizations. We know families that have simplified their lives and made real sacrifices so they can live on one paycheck. When such a decision is possible for a family, we applaud their commitment and pluck. Nevertheless, the reality is that two-parent families bringing in two incomes has become the norm.

Are Two Employed Parents Good for Children?

What *is* known about the impact of mothers' employment and day care on children? Jean Curtis interviewed many parents in preparation for her book *Working Mothers*. She began her investigation unsure of where she stood on this topic, but concluded that, for many children, the mother's working impacted children positively. The children adapted rather easily to being cared for by several adults. Children do not forget who their parents are. She discovered further that employed parents often give their children as much attentive care as people who are with their children all day long.[11] As parents know, there are many variables—the quality of the day care, the other adults in the children's lives, the flexibility and distance of the parents' work, support for emergencies such as sickness, and more.

Is it harmful for older children to provide self-care for part of the day? Hyman Rodman points out that we have too quickly fallen into negative stereotypes; even the term *latchkey child* has negative overtones. He remarks that journalists and researchers have looked for problems, have found some, which they have then generalized.

On the other hand, he points to some studies of self-care children in grades five through seven, in which the children that provide their own after-school care had no significant differences on measures of school adjustment, classroom orientation, and achievement level. He admits that there are not yet enough studies to draw widespread conclusions.

Latchkey stereotypes are common, but very little is actually known about the reality of the self-care situation and its consequences for children. . . . [therefore] it is risky to come to premature conclusions about the consequences of self-care. . . . [Quite probably] some of the early negative reports are not sufficiently cautious about the complexity of the situation.[12]

Two-Career Families Face Their Tasks

Children may be asked to make the contribution of "self-care," just as children in earlier generations independently carried out responsibilities for farm animals and chores.

Two-career families need to create a new pattern of behavior and expectation for their self-care children, working out family policies about guests, homework, TV, chores, and use of time. Self-care does not by any means exceed what children in other times and cultures contributed to their families' welfare. Support of adults who drop by and/or who can be called, ways to deal with emergencies, and more need to be planned and put into operation.

Two-career families can manage better if work environments are more family friendly. One parent might consider working part time. Or workplaces might be open to flexible time commitments, parental leave, permission to work at home when necessary, and other family-friendly policies.

It may be possible for families to band together to exchange services. Some at-home parents might provide care or oversee self-care for a number of children, for a fair wage. This could be that parent's employment and be sturdy support for a few other families.

Implications for Ministry

Two-income households are a major fact of life for congregations. Church after church is finding that parishioners' lives are crowded to overflowing with responsibilities, pressures, and tension. These families have little time to spare and church programs suffer. Often the wife-mother is working a double shift (one at the office and one at home) because men are slow to adapt to the new order. On the other hand, as we noted above, many dads are becoming important caregivers in their families, being responsible for children while mothers work. The issues facing these families are child care, scarcity of time, and conflicting pressures when jobs are demanding and children are sick or troubled.

Planning Skills

Two-career families need planning skills. One intriguing model is the Work/Family Retreat designed by Bonnie Michaels. The accompanying book, *Solving the Work Family Puzzle,* gives clues about how all families, especially those with two careers, can manage life with more joy and less frustration.[13] A retreat setting breaks with the routine and provides opportunities for fun and playful interactions across the generations. In this learning atmosphere, a couple can decide for themselves how they want to organize income-producing activities and parenting responsibilities. Whole families can explore how tasks get done in their home, how family work can be shared, and how families can build into their lives both fun and meaningful interaction. Here they can learn that all decisions are "for the time being" and can be renegotiated when a better way presents itself or as children mature and can take on new responsibilities.

Support Strategies

Congregations can be supportive to these families in some concrete ways:

- Organize a phone network for children whose parents are at work when they come home from school; recruit an older adult facilitator who likes children.

- Identify "safe houses" where youngsters can go when danger threatens in their neighborhood.

- Identify a safe corridor between home and school where adults will be watchful and available if trouble arises.

- Develop an after-school program for children and youth one or more afternoons a week; staff the program with education students from a local college and retired adults.

- Facilitate a family-to-family network for sharing child care and periodic cooperative meal preparation.

4. Ministry and the Challenge of Sexuality

Speaking credibly about sexual behavior is no small challenge for church leaders today. Many, even inside the churches, have simply turned off to what "the church" says about sex. Reports of clergy misconduct and abuse of women and children undermine the moral authority of all church leaders. Rev. Marie Fortune, a pioneer in forging a response by faith communities to the tragedy and evil of domestic violence, child abuse, and clergy misconduct, has taken on the question of what makes a sexual relationship a right relationship.[14]

Fortune has identified five compelling guidelines for relationships. First, a sexual relationship needs to be a peer relationship. This involves profoundly challenging the cultural assumption that there's something sexy about men dominating and women submitting. "What would happen," she asks,

> if equality itself was an erotic experience? The possibility of a relationship with someone who is equally strong, capable, self-confident, and clear about her/his interests and desires seems most attractive if one is really interested in a relationship: that is in spending time with someone in an experience of intimacy and trust.[15]

Friendships are more likely to be peer relationships. Good sex, sex that meets the needs and affirms the worth of both partners, happens between equals.

Second, a moral sexual relationship requires authentic consent. That means partners are in fact free to say no at any point without suffering harm. It means partners must be of legal age and be unimpaired by drugs or alcohol or psychological or mental deficiencies. One must be able to understand the consequences of sexual activity. Authentic consent means making a decision that is not pressured, coerced, made contingent on something else. It requires a high level of self-knowledge, maturity, safety, and self-confidence.

Fortune's third guideline is the stewardship of one's sexuality. By this she means taking responsibility for protecting oneself and one's partner against sexually transmitted diseases and unintended pregnancy. It means anticipating the literal consequences of one's actions. Clearly, being good stewards of our sexuality rules out one-night stands and casual relationships. It presumes committed partnership in which trust has developed.

A fourth guideline is sharing sexual pleasure. The commitment to the partner's needs has to be as significant as the concern to meet one's own. This involves developing a truly intimate relationship in which it is safe and comfortable for partners to express their needs and desires—to be honest about what is pleasurable. Fortune quotes Mary Hunt, a feminist theologian: "Sex for some people is no more intimate than fast food, just another commodity which can be bought or bartered." Fortune goes on to observe, "In this instance, sexual activity loses its erotic quality that grounds us in the meaning of life and life together."[16] Those who have read the "Song of Songs" know better!

Faithfulness is the fifth guideline to a sexual relationship of integrity. Faithfulness means keeping promises and commitments whatever their nature or duration. It means being truthful with each other about our feelings and intentions. It also means being truthful with our community. Intimate relationships do not survive "in the closet," out of sight of the community that provides support, a reality check, or a challenge. If we have promised monogamy, faithfulness means being monogamous. As a practical matter, Fortune reminds us, monogamy is not only an extension of our religious values; it is a means of staying alive. Faithfulness also means paying attention to our partner, investing prime time in the relationship. Failing to pay attention to our partner and allowing everything else in life to crowd out our relationship is probably the most common form of adultery! Finally, faithfulness means no violence in the relationship. Where violence or the threat of violence occurs, the covenant is broken, trust is betrayed, and intimacy is destroyed.

Concern about Teen Sexual Activity

In terms of sexuality, when church leaders and parents ponder what moral guidance to give the young these days, there are new factors to consider:

The meaning people invest in sexual activity has shifted. Sharing a sexual experience with another used to be mysterious and very special. For many today it seems just another form of communication, no big deal.

Culture, particularly media, has encouraged this view of sex. All too often it has given a distorted view of recreational, amoral, sex-without-consequences. There is little help from the media in communicating a wholesome, spiritual, joyous view of sex.

Children and youths are caught up in these trends. Every survey points in the direction of earlier and more widespread involvement in sexual activity among the young.

AIDS makes all the difference in the world. Unprotected sexual activity can be fatal. Young adults in their twenties who are afflicted with AIDS contracted it in their midteens. Unlike previous generations, sexual experimentation during the teen years can kill.

Another grave concern is the issue of pregnancy among teens. Judy Root Aulette's documented observations are important in this regard. She notes that between 1955 and 1988 the adolescent fertility rate dropped by 41 percent (45 percent for Whites, 37 percent for Blacks). At the same time, concern about adolescent pregnancy and childbearing has grown. She feels the attention and concern comes from several quarters. For one thing, in the fifties pregnant teens could be/were expelled from school and thus became more invisible. Now they are visible in schools. Then many soon married; now very few do. Further, while the fertility rate of teenagers has declined, it has not declined as fast as the rate for nonteens. She notes also that while the birthrate has declined, the rate of pregnancy of woman aged fifteen to nineteen has grown, from 82.1 per thousand women in 1973 to 96 per thousand in 1981. The difference between pregnancy and birthrate is due to the higher numbers of abortions. About one-quarter of all abortions in U.S. are for women under the age of nineteen.[17]

In a similar vein, Kristin Luker suggests,

Teen pregnancy is less about young women and their sex lives than it is about restricted horizons and the boundaries of hope. It is about race and class and how those realities limit opportunities for young people. Most centrally, however, it is typically about being young, female, poor, and non-white and about how having a child seems to be one of the few avenues of satisfaction, fulfillment, and self-esteem.

It would be a tragedy to stop worrying about these young women—and their partners—because their behavior is the measure rather than the cause of their blighted hopes.[18]

Marian Wright Edelman suggests that the way to prevent teen pregnancy is "give them hope, opportunity, information and skills." This includes "Many and varied opportunities for success. . . . Building academic skills. . . . Work-related skill-building and work exposure. . . . Family-life education and life planning. . . . Comprehensive adolescent health services. . . ."[19]

Our Message to Young People

There is much wisdom in these insights that teen sexual activity and pregnancy may well have causes in despair and hopelessness, and these certainly should be addressed. Even as we agree with them, we are not off the hook as to what moral guidance to offer children, youth, and young adults on sexual matters. Here are a few things we would include in that guidance:

•   Programs and movements by church groups encouraging young people to abstain from intercourse until marriage have recently received much publicity. True Love Waits from the Southern Baptist youth department is one of the best known. We think efforts that encourage young people to postpone sexual intimacy have considerable merit.

•   But there is more that must be said to young people about responsible sex than simply "wait." A marriage license does not automatically make a sexual relationship a right relationship. The guidelines suggested by Marie Fortune are an eloquent statement of what must be shared with young people.

•   Parents have a critical role to play. No one can bless a youngster's sexuality with more power than a parent. No affirmation of one's femaleness or maleness is as healing and strengthening as that given by our parents. Parents need to evaluate their own sexual experiences, ask themselves searching questions, and communicate to their children: What sexual experiences do they hope their children will have? What sexual experiences do they hope their children will avoid? What will help prepare them for a life-long, committed sexual relationship? We know it is difficult for parents and children to think of each other as sexual beings, but the conversation needs to be attempted.

• A new-old repertoire of romantic sexual experiences without genital expression may need to be communicated. Think in terms of a couple of pamphlets we've seen: *What to Do While You Wait* and *101 Things to Do instead of Doing It.*

• Parents, churches, and educational systems need to team together for wide-ranging discussion and education on these topics. The information we have studied indicates there are sex education courses that are effective in reducing the amount of sexual involvement among young people. These are courses that provide full information, including information about contraceptives and sexually transmitted diseases. These courses also give ample attention and training in decision-making and refusal skills.

The Critical Importance of Adult Sexuality Education

The faith community does have something helpful to say about sexuality. It needs to be said, however, at the grassroots by the people of the faith community, rather than through pronouncements from remote "authorities." We can restore credibility in what the church says about sexuality as we provoke and nurture conversation in local congregations. We believe that sexuality education is not primarily a matter of teaching the facts to youth. We believe sexuality education needs to begin with adults. Adults set the tone of a congregation. If they can talk about sexual issues in church, then young people will too.

Research shows that parents are the most powerful sexuality educators. Children whose parents make sure they discuss sexual issues as a regular part of family conversation grow up to be adolescents who value sexual restraint and delay beginning sexual activity, as compared with children whose parents stay silent about sexuality. Congregations can equip parents for their important role.

The pressures on young people to be sexual and to identify with sexualized media images is enormous. Girls, especially, beginning with junior high, are at risk for everything from anorexia and depression to pregnancy and suicide because of the expectations pressed upon them by media and peer youth culture. Boys are being powerfully socialized, largely by media, to exploit and demean girls.[20] Adults need to be strong guarantors and protectors. They need to be vigorous advocates for changing the ways boys and girls are socialized in our churches, schools, and in the youth culture. One parent of one son or daughter can not do it alone. Congregations are places where parents can become informed, share the pain they are experiencing with their adolescents, and create culture-transforming strategies.

Humans at every stage of development have sexual issues. Sexual education needs to be a life-long process. What better place than the church for such education to take place? Our heritage of Scripture tells us that our sexuality is God-created and good and that right relationships among us include disciplining our sexual impulses and energy. Our Scripture even includes an erotic poem! We must accept the challenge to create a congregational climate in which deep reflection and conversation about sexual issues can happen. Out of such a climate can come an authentic, credible word about what is valuable in sexual relationships, what is distorted, and how we can tell the difference.

Implications for Ministry

Adult Education

Congregations can get started when a few leaders take the risk to begin planning. Begin with low-risk strategies: an adult class on human sexuality or a book study that deals with the Bible and sexuality or a study circle on gender issues. Add parent sexuality education to help parents become more informed and comfortable talking about sexual issues, first with each other and then with their children. Encourage parents to talk with your congregation's educational planners about the values they hope to instill in their children. Train teachers and others who work with children and youth in the congregation to recognize the symptoms of sexual abuse and how they can respond when a child or youth discloses an abusive experience or relationship. Be sure to include an opportunity for members to learn about aging and sexuality.

As educational approaches take hold, consider how sexual issues can be dealt with in worship. You might begin with a worship series that lifts up the gifts of women and men. Another season you might ask the pastor to explore the "Song of Songs" in a sermon or in a Bible study series; this poetical affirmation of our bodies and of our sexuality needs to be heard in the church! In worship prophetically address the tension points in contemporary society and challenge the culture's distortions of sexuality.

Education for Children and Youth

Only after adults have become more open and capable of dealing with sexual issues can a congregation meaningfully consider sexuality education of children and youth. Begin by offering sexuality education units in your Christian education program to children and youth. Include sexual abuse prevention in the curriculum (see resources). Be sure preadolescents learn refusal skills, decision-making skills, and good social skills. Do everything to encourage self-esteem and self-respect. Children who are less able to relate to their peers and who feel badly about themselves are at greater risk for exploitation as the pressure to belong grows through adolescence. A well-stocked church library of books and videos on sexual issues provides a real service to children, youth, and their families.

With older youth and young adults, raise the issue of date rape. Facilitate conversations about Marie Fortune's five guidelines and focus especially on authentic consent. Confront young people with the statistics that show how very many young women feel pressured into sexual activity.[21] Help young women make clear to young men what coercion looks like and feels like from their perspective.

Young people also need to learn how to evaluate media messages. There are resources, for both peer education and intergenerational settings, for learning how to watch television critically (see resources). You might explore the message of youth-oriented music, dress styles, and the reality of fads as commercial manipulation.

Move into Community Service

Congregations that hope to impact the culture around them can do so through outreach programs. If your congregation's facility is on the route of children going and coming from school, consider a drop-in center with a trusted adult team available to talk and appropriate literature to share. Organize a telephone hotline to function a few hours a week with trained peer counselors who can answer questions about sexuality and other adolescent concerns. Consider doing a cable television program or series on sexual messages in the media; educate your community. You might want to team up with another congregation or a helping agency, such as the Y, a mental health center, or a family service agency.

Other strategies that will raise the consciousness of the congregation and the community: fund raising for a rape crisis center; giving a platform to young people choosing abstinence; advocating for comprehensive sexuality education in the schools. Congregations can offer the community a course in critical television viewing or organize a forum with local broadcasters to discuss community standards.

5. Ministry and the Challenge of Cohabitation

We have already discussed some of the facts about cohabitation. Increasingly both religious and secular pundits are arguing for a recommitment to the institution of marriage, claiming that those who cohabit have a 50 percent higher likelihood of divorce than those who don't. Michael McManus counsels pastors to require cohabiting couples desiring a church wedding to separate first.[22] This, he believes, will reduce the likelihood of later divorce. Would that it were so simple!

Recent Research on Cohabitation

So far as we have been able to discover, no studies of cohabitation have turned up evidence that it contributes to a better marriage. All of the early studies we found conclude that cohabitation in fact leads to greater marital instability. But a recent study by Robert Schoen has challenged the claim that cohabitants are at greater risk for divorce if and when they marry.[23] Working with data from the National Survey of Families and

Households, Schoen looked carefully at couples married up to ten years in different age cohorts. (A cohort is the class of people born in a specified time period, for example between 1940 and 1945 or between 1960 and 1965.) He compared the rates of marital dissolution (divorce or separation) of cohabitants in each cohort with the dissolution rates of noncohabitants in the same cohort. As expected, he found that for people born in the twenties through the early fifties, cohabitants had a higher rate of marital dissolution. But this differential declined and even reversed for those born in the late fifties. He reasons that as cohabitation becomes more wide-spread and less exceptional, the differences between cohabitants and noncohabitants will decrease considerably.

Another recent study is also relevant. Alfred DeMaris and William McDonald also looked at the National Survey of Families and Households and asked whether cohabiting couples who married reported greater marital instability than noncohabitants who married.[24] They measured instability by asking questions such as, In the past year, has your marriage been in trouble? Have you thought about divorce or separation in the past year? Do you think that eventually your marriage will end in divorce?

This study sorted out those who cohabited only with the person they married (single-instance cohabitants) from those who cohabited with several partners (serial cohabitants). They found that single-instance cohabitants reported no more marital instability than couples who had never cohabited. Only serial cohabitants report more marital instability than noncohabitants. DeMaris and McDonald reason that those who have made a commitment to cohabit and then broken it are more likely to do the same in a marriage. Those who made a commitment to cohabit and kept that commitment are likely to keep their commitment to marriage.

Insights and Dilemmas

We propose that choosing to live together even without a wedding is a commitment. Looking at cohabitation in light of Fortune's guidelines for a moral sexual relationship gives us a way of evaluating a specific relationship. What promises has the couple made to each other? Are they being honest with each other? Is the relationship between peers, and is it authentically consensual? Is it a closeted relationship, or is it known to the couple's community?

Ministry to cohabiting couples may well mean first of all challenging them to be explicit about the promises they are making and to connect with their community. One of Joe's young friends, talking about how he met his wife, said, "We thought we would just live together. But her parents were not comfortable with that, and we were ready to make the commitment. So we got married."

We also note that many young people enter a cohabitational relationship in good faith, to test the relationship. Living together has become a stage in courtship. It is sometimes driven by economic concerns. It does offer an opportunity for a couple to discover how they handle the vicissitudes of daily life. It need not be a sexual relationship. Listen to this young married woman:

> After graduating, I got a job in Washington D.C. and Ken moved there so that we could pursue our relationship. We ended up sharing an apartment with another college friend. He and Ken shared a bedroom and I had the other. Our commitment to sexual intercourse within marriage made our living situation even more unusual. Many warned us of the risks we were taking. One insightful comment was that we would face much of the work of marriage without a significant part of the joy. I better understand now the challenge we confidently undertook. Yet, it was in the "work of marriage" that I became more sure that I could marry Ken. I watched him take out the trash, wash dishes, and always come up with his third of the rent. I learned that he was willing to negotiate, able to affirm my gifts and skills, and was good-natured in tough situations. I realized that I had found in Ken a companion, a friend, and a lover of the truest kind. I have learned that marriage is not so much about finding the right person as about building the right relationship. And I knew that I could trust Ken to build alongside me.[25]

This topic needs attention in family discussions of sexuality. It needs to be considered long before a couple comes home announcing that they have moved in together. Family values about such matters need to be discussed and family policies explored. For example, many families have faced questions: Do we continue to provide assistance for education if our children cohabit? If they decide to do so, is the couple welcome in our home? One bedroom or two?

Those considering cohabitation should be aware that our society as a whole has unclear attitudes about this practice. Insurance, property ownership, and more can be complicating factors for the cohabiting unmarried couple.

Implications for Ministry

Pastoral Concerns

When it comes to cohabiting couples, churches need to be clear in their attitudes and policies. Are cohabiting couples welcome in worship? In membership? In leadership? We advocate for welcome into the life and membership of the church. At the same time, given the wide range of attitudes in many congregations, we suggest caution in putting these folks in "role model" positions such as teachers of children or advisors of youth groups. That, however, is a decision each church must make for itself.

At the same time, church leaders need to be aware that they too have a burden of proof for credibility on these issues. Many people see little value or significance in a religious wedding—or a civil one for that matter. What do we in the church believe a wedding to be? What do we believe it contributes to a couple's life together? Have we invested the integrity and dignity in it to undergird what we say we believe? Clergy and couples—all, not just cohabiting couples—owe each other the gifts of honesty and candor. Enduring marriage is under siege these days. A foundation from which to start is honesty about what is this marriage bond and the ritual by which we celebrate it.

As a pastor, I (Dick) have worked with many cohabiting couples planning weddings. I do not feel that ministers need to ask cohabiting couples to live apart while preparing for a wedding. But premarital cohabitation does need to be on the table in premarital counseling. What have you learned about self, other, and the way you live life together? What are you hoping will change as you marry and commit your lives to each other? What have you been postponing talking about until after the wedding? As you move from one level of commitment to another, what new covenants do you wish to make with each other?

Ministry with cohabiting couples is complicated by the fact that their behavior contradicts "official" church teachings about connecting marriage and sexuality. Consequently, it is not talked about in church, aside from occasional denunciation. Many pastors are confused themselves, having children who are cohabiting or did cohabit before they married. It is difficult to pronounce on an issue when one's experience seems to run counter to "official" dogma. Nevertheless, we are not comfortable simply blessing cohabitation and announcing that the traditional restriction of sexual expression to legal, religiously sanctioned relationships should be abandoned. Our respect for the spiritual and psychological potential of the sexual bond is too great to reduce sexual intercourse to a recreational or casual pursuit. And the central issue, whether a couple is cohabiting or marrying, or remarrying, is commitment.

Ministry to Parents

Older parents whose adult children are cohabiting may need sensitive support from pastors and from other parents experiencing the same thing. Jokes about how to refer to the cohabiting partner when introducing one's grown child and the partner reveal our uneasiness. Here is an intimate relationship for which we have no name. And while a parent may refer with a smile to a grown child "living in sin," the joking reference could be a cover for disappointment. Some opportunity to share feelings and share experiences with other parents may be all that's needed. Parents can teach one another ways to respond to their young adult children.

A second group of parents are those whose children are nearing young adulthood. For them, the issues of cohabitation may be more complex, especially if they cohabited before their own marriage. There are parents who will expect this behavior, may even recommend it to their children. There will also be parents who cohabited but regretted it later. We believe it is important for parents in a congregation to talk with one another about these experiences in a nonblaming atmosphere. What have they learned and how can this be passed on to the next generation? What do they want their young people taught about cohabitation? Are there shared values among parents related to promise making and keeping, consent, equality in relationships, nonexploitation, and faithfulness? Such shared values, once identified, can become the foundation for ethical reflection and teaching in the congregation.

Ministry with Cohabiting Couples

Cohabiting young people are often absent from church. They show up when they have finally decided to marry. Ministry with them may need to be, in the beginning, ministry to their parents. But the issue of commitment, and the ethical value of encouraging commitments to be made in community, drive us to challenge congregations to consider when such nonmarital commitments may be ritualized. If what has emerged is a new stage in courtship or a form of limited-duration marriage, would it not be healthier for couples, their families, and their congregations to recognize this relationship in a public way? The growing gap between sexual maturity and the social, vocational, and economic readiness to found a family in a complex society needs to be dealt with in an orderly and serious way.

People who have been previously married, as we have said, represent the largest class of cohabitants. Many of the issues they face are much like those of any blended family, especially if children are present in the household. Reaching out to them as part of ministry with blended families is certainly appropriate. Functionally they are a couple and including them in couple-oriented events may be a way to establish a positive relationship. On the basis of such a relationship, you might create the space in which to explore where the couple is in relation to remarriage. Has healing from a previous marriage taken place? Are they falling into dysfunctional patterns of relationship from the past that block making appropriate public commitments to each other?

Ministry to Youth and Young Adults

We owe young people honesty about sexuality and relationships, including an honest discussion of cohabitation. They deserve to know that there is no social scientific evidence so far that it improves later marriage. The likelihood that serial cohabitation leads to divorce needs to be brought home. Young people can be helped enormously by the sincere testimonies of married people about what sexual fulfillment is, what decisions they made in their courting days and why, and how they have dealt with sexual issues in their relationship. If a congregation is prepared to recognize some cohabitational relationships, perhaps even ritualizing them, young people need to know on what basis.

If we sound protective or defensive, it is because the stakes are so high. Our culture has so little compunction about exploiting sexuality to sell products to young people. The church, in being so negative about sexuality, has lost credibility with perhaps the majority of the younger generation. Our challenge is to shape a vision of healthy sexual expression. It will be rooted in mutuality and authentic consent, based on equality, respect for self and the partner. It will affirm appreciation for our bodies of many shapes, sizes, and colors. Further, it will acknowledge that sexual activity is fun, pleasurable, mysterious, and a celebration of the deepest commitment two humans can make to each other.

6. Ministry and the Challenge of Longevity

Observers of the changing family scene point out a most pressing issue: the loneliness and need of many elderly family members. Some of these folks live at great distance from kin that could provide regular assistance. With the growing life expectancy, the *children* of many elderly folks are old enough not to have the strength or energy to provide for their parents' needs.

Faced with the needs of elderly members, families respond in a variety of ways. Some feel they must uproot them and bring them to their own homes or homes for the elderly in their own communities. Others find ways to allow their older members to stay in their life-long communities.

There is a call and an opportunity for church and families to enter into partnership on behalf of isolated, lonely elderly people.

A Revealing Case Study

In midlife Tom Koch took a leave of absence and came home to care for his father through the course of a final geriatric illness. At times he had help, and at times interference, from other members of the family. As he looked back on his experience after his father died, he analyzed how his family and community could have worked together more effectively, providing better care with less stress.

For one thing, they could have reduced or eliminated many problems if they had done one difficult but necessary task— anticipate and plan, rather than react. They needed better knowledge of and contact with their father's treasured friends in the community and his medical team; they needed to know their father's wishes for any of the eventualities they could anticipate.

Further, they needed a clear sense of the range of responsibilities that go with providing care. Those responsibilities could then have been delegated and divided. Koch feels the following division would have served his family well: (1) the primary caregiver—the one who provides the daily medical and home maintenance; (2) the financial surrogate— the one who knows the range of financial resources and how the father wants them used; (3) the legal surrogate—one who would learn from the father about legal affairs—what arrangements have already been made through what attorney; (4) the medical surrogate—one who works with the father to enter into partnership with his medical team, one who is trusted by that team with information; (5) the community surrogate—one who keeps community friends and organizations informed and involved; (6) the relations surrogate—one who keeps relatives over the miles informed and lets them know how they can be helpfully involved.[26]

One person may well take responsibility for more than one of those roles, but that is the range of responsibilities needing attention, in Koch's opinion, to care for a family member through a geriatric illness. Of course, families may divide the duties differently. In one family, the daughter who lived in the same community provided the bulk of this care. Other family members were sensitive to the strain on her and filled in regularly to give her rest and time away.

Implications for Ministry

A New Role for the Congregation?

The church, perhaps through a staff member or a sensitive member and friend of the older person, may enter into this partnership and help the family. This requires skill in forming an alliance with the older person and the scattered family members involved in a decision. At times folks in Dick's church have been dismayed at the decisions made by family members for an older person without asking any of that person's friends, clergy, or fellow church members—people who know the older adult and his or her needs, perhaps better than the quick-visit family member. There may be need for the church's role to grow larger for older people isolated from their families. With the increased age span, the frailty of the later years, and the geographical spread of families, new sensitivities and strategies are part of our ethical mandate.

Many congregations have been graying for several decades now. But so is the country, and neglect of older family members has become a self-defeating posture for congregations. Ministry can take the form of support, missional involvement, facilitation of planning by families, and forming family-congregational covenants.

Support Ministries

Most older people who need care are receiving it from family members. Why not support these families with a support circle? For the care-giving family it could provide emotional support, a sounding board for their concerns, the collective wisdom of committed friends, respite, advice about financial management, and a partner/advocate for dealing with the inevitable bureaucratic tangles that come when human services are needed. It could also provide social outlets for family and for the elderly member. For the elder, a support circle provides a space where he or she can be helped to state or clarify self-perceptions, personal needs, and wishes.

For less infirm elderly, we advise support ministries through peer groups—in which people can reminisce, celebrate anniversaries and commiserate the foibles of one's children and grandchildren, mourn when death comes to a member of one's circle. The existing structure of organized classes, circles, and study groups typical of many congregations can evolve into support groups for elderly members. Retreats and camp and conference opportunities are effective and appreciated by this group of members.

Missional Ministries

Recently retired folks often have an abundance of energy, wisdom, and drive waiting to be tapped. The wise leader will help those folks become engaged in mission. Short-term assignments are often available through denominational volunteer offices. Skills in teaching, mentoring, administering, accounting, managing, and publicizing can be useful to community nonprofit organizations, denominational educational institutions, and overseas.

A group of seniors in Joe's church organized themselves into a "senior support corps." This group has two focuses: to support each other and to be a support to many missional enterprises of the congregation and community. Members of the group have volunteered to drive a visiting African choir on its tour of several states. Others have spent time in Caribbean villages, helping a traveling doctor and nurse with their round of clinics. Many regularly volunteer their labor to an international relief organization with a nearby warehouse shipping facility.

Planning Ministries

As we age, we all should make decisions about how we want to spend our last days. The wise congregation offers opportunities for elders to explore these questions. Wise, too, is the congregation that equips families to network their extended kin in organizing support for aging parents. Retirement communities can provide leadership for retreats or workshops exploring with seniors the kinds of arrangements they want to make for their last years. Planned giving counselors from denominational foundations are equipped to help elders consider their legacy and how they can support causes dear to them after they have ended their pilgrimage. Book studies of writings such as Tom Koch's, referenced above, can help both elders and the middle-aged anticipate and prepare for the decisions and arrangements that come with aging. And having heard older members complain about the preacher's habit of reading a favorite paraphrase of Psalm 23 at *every* memorial service leads us to suggest a participatory workshop for older folks on "what I want (and don't want) in my memorial service."

Covenanting Ministries

Older members of a congregation may live a good distance away from children and other relatives. Their church friends may well know them better and have a clearer sense of their wishes than distant relatives. Why not offer seniors and their distant families an opportunity to covenant with the congregation for the care of an aging member? A support circle of friends that is also open to participation by a relative could be the means of making one's last days good days.

All these strategies increase the choice, control, and support that older people can have over their own lives, even as their capacity for decision and action wanes.

7. Ministry and the Challenge of Gay and Lesbian Christians

I (Joe) belong to an American Baptist congregation that for at least twenty-five years has welcomed into its membership and leadership gay and lesbian Christians. This has simply been the congregation's practice. More recently, as the inclusion of gay and lesbian Christians has become a contentious issue for congregations and denominations, we have begun to be public about our practice and to deal with it theologically. For example, the board of Christian education sponsored three conversations among parents, board members, and representatives of the mission group that focused on the issues and concerns facing sexual minority people. These conversations discussed what we want to teach our children and youth about human relationships, sexuality, and covenantal partnerships. Could we reach a consensus around basic values we want to share with our children and youth? We have a tradition of sexuality education programs for youth and adults, so these conversations were not extraordinary.

We identified a number of values: that all human beings are created by God as sexual beings, and that sexual orientation is part of the created nature of human beings. Our sexuality is God's gift, to be enjoyed and expressed responsibly. Our bodies are good and deserving of care and respect. A sexual relationship is a wonderful human good when it is characterized by mutual consent and equality and when it takes place in a context of tender caring and enduring commitment. We affirmed enduring, monogamous partnerships as an ideal we want our children to strive for and that we adults of whatever sexual orientation seek to model. Indeed, one of the gifts brought by gay and lesbian couples in our membership was the stimulus for heterosexual couples to reflect more deeply on what it means to be committed to an enduring, monogamous partnership!

These conversations occurred during a time when the whole congregation focused on the biblical and theological issues raised by the reality of differing sexual orientations. Our pastor preached on the theme and presented a theological position paper. A noted biblical scholar led an adult forum. These activities were undertaken to enable members to sort out the issues and clarify their individual views. The congregation sponsored a resolution on the need for denominational dialogue about human sexuality, calling for an atmosphere of tolerance for and genuine listening to differing points of view. The resolution, watered down of course, was eventually adopted by the general board of our denomination.

We certainly recognize that Joe's congregation is not "typical" in its response to the presence of gay and lesbian Christians. Its response is, however, consistent with its history. Throughout its first hundred years, the congregation has repeatedly identified itself with marginalized people and their causes. For example, during the 1980s the congregation voted to be a "sanctuary church" for undocumented Central Americans and housed several in its building during a time when the legality of doing so was being questioned. Advocating for those whose rights are being abused or who are facing discrimination is central to the way this congregation does ministry.

Implications for Ministry

Note that gay and lesbian couples and families need many of the same kinds of family ministry as do their heterosexual brothers and sisters. Retreats for couples to work on their relationship, parenting education, and communication-skills training are equally relevant to gay and lesbian Christian families.

We also offer this caveat: Do not assume that two people of the same gender sharing a household are involved sexually. A single mother in Joe's congregation lives with a woman friend in a covenantal relationship that is not sexual. While they accept same-sex couples who are sexual, they are offended when folks jump to conclusions about their relationship. Being open to ministry with same-gender couples does not always mean ministry with gay and lesbian people. It means, rather, giving people the space and respect to define themselves and their relational commitments.

Three Steps a Congregation Might Take

For many congregations, acknowledging the reality of human sexuality in church is challenging enough, to say nothing of discussing the spectrum of sexual orientations. For many congregations, offering opportunities for adults, youth, and children to learn about human sexuality in the church would be a great step forward. Only religious communities can ground sexuality education in an appreciation for it as one of God's gifts. The church can also uniquely interpret human sexuality in ways that lift up its relation to spirituality and critique its consumerist and exploitative distortions typical of popular culture. This is the first step we would urge upon all congregations.

A second step is to raise awareness that gay and lesbian people have been and are contributors to the well being of communities in every part of the world. Leaders, especially pastoral leaders, need to help congregations sort out popular cultural stereotypes and attitudes toward sexual minorities from genuine Christian theological understandings of human sexuality. Education includes informing members about the realities of life for people whose orientation is other than simply heterosexual. Allies in this effort will be the parents, siblings, and sons and daughters of gay and lesbian people who are part of your congregation. A typical congregation probably includes gay and lesbian members—who must hide their orientation to protect their jobs, relationships, and even physical security. You can and should help the congregation empathize with those who live under such oppression. Of course at some point, pastoral leaders will have to deal with a few passages of Scripture that are frequently interpreted as condemning gay and lesbian people. But Jesus' pattern of reaching out to those regarded as "unclean," immoral, and outside God's concern provides a strong biblical basis for including sexual minority

people in the life of the church. In this process of education, a congregation can recall and celebrate the times it has reached out to other marginalized people and groups.

We recommend a third step for congregations that are seeking the
mind of Christ about how they can be welcoming, safe, and affirming
places for Christians who are gay or lesbian: Create small-group dialogue between self-affirming Christians who are gay and lesbian and
congregational members. Most denominations now have sexual minority
caucuses or associations that can help this to happen without putting gay
and lesbian congregants on the spot with fellow church members. In the
present climate in many communities, the social, psychological, and
physical safety of gay and lesbian people has to be a concern for congregations actively struggling with the issues raised by Christians who are
gay and lesbian.

Begin with Parents and Grandparents

We have already pointed out how congregations can begin to minister
with same-gender families by educating themselves. A good starting
point for both education and ministry is to parents and grandparents of
lesbian and gay children. However people come to be homosexually
oriented, it happens to conservatives and fundamentalists, to liberals and
radicals, to Republicans and Democrats without favor or distinction!
The parents and grandparents of gay and lesbian people, having been
socialized in a heterosexist culture, probably have a lot to work through.
Congregations can provide caring and tender support, sound information,
and the opportunity to dialogue with others in the same situation. Connecting them with organizations such as Parents and Friends of Lesbians
and Gays (P-FLAG) is important (see resources). These parents and
grandparents can be leaven in the congregation, challenging stereotypes
and prejudiced comments, gently educating and putting a human face on
an issue so often discussed in dehumanizing terms.

Inclusive Strategies

Same-gender couples, as we have said, have many of the same relational issues as opposite-sex couples. Where same-sex are comfortable relating with opposite-sex couples, for example in a communication workshop for couples, include them. If it is safe for same-gender couples to be out in your congregation, they can help surface important issues of what we mean by commitment, faithfulness, equality, and mutuality in intimate relationships. Include them in dialogue about these issues, and enlist their help in educating parents about how to deal with the reality of homosexuality as their children ask questions. It is highly probable that at least one young person growing up in a congregation is same-sex oriented. What a help to this young person to know a couple in the congregation that are living in a committed relationship! To have such a healthy role model of commitment and maturity could easily make the difference in the young person's life between depression and self-confidence.

Ritual

A few inclusive congregations have begun to ritualize same-gender commitments. Such rituals have value in bringing into the light of day a relationship that could otherwise be closeted, unsupported, and ungrounded in community. Ritual affords the local faith community the opportunity to express public support to the couple and celebrate the couple's commitment and love. This kind of affirmation by a congregation can bring healing and strength to the families of the same-gender couple—families that are probably having to take an unplanned, uncharted journey. See the resources for information about where to find examples of same-gender commitment rituals.

Ongoing Support

Ongoing support for same-gender couples needs to be provided—as for opposite-gender couples. This may mean support groups specifically for these couples, in which they have opportunities to deal with whatever issues may be special to a same-sex couple. Even if these couples are entirely integrated into the couple support system of a congregation, an occasional retreat or workshop especially for them is probably helpful.

A congregation open to homosexually oriented people will need a support system where both gay and straight can work together educating, interpreting, and advocating. A mission group or task force focused on the needs of gay and lesbian believers is required, especially in the climate that pervades both church and society today. The educational task is enduring. As a congregation becomes inclusive, it will experience its own "coming out" process. It will have to make decisions about how public it is about its stance and what role it will play in denominational life. A mission group or task force can undergird and guide this process of self-education and public witness.

Conclusion

In this chapter we have responded to seven challenges brought to us by contemporary families. We have answered from within a framework of family support. We offered a vision of ministry that respects family agenda and seeks to evaluate church program from the standpoint of its contribution to family wholeness. It is time for congregations to rethink how they "do church." No greater gift could be offered to contemporary families than the presence of a supportive spiritual community. May your congregation learn to be so!

A Closing Word of Encouragement and Hope

All of this information—about needs, crises, issues, strategies, possible ministries—may feel overwhelming. Faced with so many needs and possibilities, it may be hard to discover the one or two good things that a church can do to enrich family lives.

And so we will suggest a few basic steps to help a leader or a church sort out the information we've provided and arrive at some decisions. Perhaps an individual will do this alone. If you are a pencil-and-paper person, sketch out your thoughts in response to the following paragraphs, one at a time. Some church groups may want to read and discuss the book together, having someone summarize the group's thoughts (including responses to the questions below) on chalkboard or newsprint. Reflective readers may find themselves asking many questions about families in their communities to which they do not know the answers. That is to be expected and is "okay." At least someone is beginning to notice and care about a particular family group!

In chapter 1 we listed the prominent elements of change impacting families. Reflect. Do all the cited changes apply in your community? Some more, some less? What else is going on in your community that impacts families?

In chapter 2 we discussed the changing landscape of families—divorce, single parents, remarriages, unmarried cohabitation. Do these exist in your community? In your church? In the same proportion in your church as in the community? Have church leaders identified ministry opportunities with each of these groups?

We also spoke of families under stress. Do family members in your congregation or community reveal signs of these stresses? Of resilience?

In chapter 3 we outlined a number of biblical-theological insights that informed us. Did that list feel convincing to you? What would you add to it? Subtract from it?

In chapter 4 we presented five basic dimensions of family ministry. If you were to pick one of these to emphasize and explore for the coming year, which would it be? What would you like to see happen in that area? What possible steps could you take?

In chapter 5 we discussed seven contemporary challenges to family ministry. Are you actively ministering in some of these areas? Of the remaining, which might require preparation and slow entry? Which is your church ready to consider right now? In what one area would you like to take some forward steps?

When you stop listening to us and start reflecting on your own ministry, we suspect you'll encounter some surprises, discovering: (1) how much you and your church are already doing; (2) how much these changes are already part of the people in your church; (3) the reservoir of goodwill and caring that exists among church folk, willing to reach out in family ministries—when they see the way; (4) the mission opportunity that lurks in some of the family types we have discussed.

Because of the rapid changes over the last seven years, we were glad for the opportunity to write an update of our previous book on ministry with changing families. And yet the moment this book goes to press, it becomes frozen in time. Given the nature of our subject, much of it will very shortly be out of date. The sequels to this book will be the people and churches who take a clue or two from it and find ways to reach out in love to the many-faceted families around them. With joy we anticipate that the latter story will be greater than the former; your story will be more exciting than ours! Go to it, and may God richly bless your every effort on behalf of families.

NOTES

Chapter 1

1. Loren Mead, *The Once and Future Church* (Bethesda, Md.: The Alban Institute, 1991), v.

2. Monica McGoldrick, "Ethnicity, Cultural Diversity, and Normality," in *Normal Family Processes,* ed. Froma Walsh, 2nd ed. (New York: Guilford Press, 1993), 331-33.

3. Wallace Charles Smith, *The Church in the Life of the Black Family* (Valley Forge, Pa.: Judson Press, 1985).

4. Quoted in Arlene Skolnick, *Embattled Paradise: The American Family in an Age of Uncertainty* (New York: HarperCollins, Basic Books, 1991), 60.

5. Quoted in ibid., 47.

6. Ibid., 8.

7. Judy Root Aulette, *Changing Families* (Belmont, Calif.: Wadsworth, 1994), 113.

8. Stephanie Coontz, *The Way We Never Were: American Families and the Nostalgia Trap* (New York: HarperCollins, Basic Books, 1992), 263-65; Aulette, *Changing Families,* 91.

9. Coontz, *The Way We Never Were,* 264.

10. Quoted in Maxine Baca Zinn and D. Stanley Eitzen, *Diversity in Families* (New York: Harper & Row, 1990), 432.

11. Marian Wright Edelman, "Leave No Child Behind," *Church and Society* 84, no. 2 (November-December 1993): 133-43.

12. Peter Uhlenberg, "Death and the Family," in *Family in Transition: Rethinking Marriage, Sexuality, Childrearing and Family Organization,*

ed. Arlene S. Skolnick and Jerome H. Skolnick, 7th ed. (New York: HarperCollins, 1992), 72-81.

13. Thomas B. Robb, "Aging and Ageism: Implications for the Church's Ministry with Families," *Church and Society* 84, no. 2: 190-21; Paul C. Glick, "American Families: As They Are and Were," in *Family in Transition: Rethinking Marriage, Sexuality, Childrearing and Family Organization,* ed. Arlene S. Skolnick and Jerome H. Skolnick, 7th ed. (New York: HarperCollins, 1992), 93.

14. Russell Chandler, *Racing toward 2001* (Grand Rapids: Zondervan, 1992), 36.

15. Skolnick and Skolnick, "Introduction," 15.

16. Joel Crohn, *Mixed Matches: How to Create Successful Interracial, Interethnic, and Interfaith Relationships* (New York: Fawcett Columbine, 1995).

17. Lenore J. Weitzman and Ruth B. Dixon, "The Transformation of Legal Marriage through No-Fault Divorce," in *Family in Transition: Rethinking Marriage, Sexuality, Childrearing and Family Organization,* ed. Arlene S. Skolnick and Jerome H. Skolnick, 7th ed. (New York: HarperCollins, 1992), 218–26.

18. Aulette, *Changing Families,* 295-96.

19. Fred M. Hechinger, *Fateful Choices: Healthy Youth for the Twenty-First Century* (New York: Farrar, Straus and Giroux, Hill and Wang, 1992), 21-22.

20. Ibid., 53–54.

21. Alan Guttmacher Institute, *Sex and America's Teenagers* (New York: Alan Guttmacher Institute, 1994); Sue Woodman, "How Teenage Pregnancy Has Become a Political Football," *MS* 4 (January-February 1995): 90.

22. Hechinger, *Fateful Choices,* 165.

23. James Dobson and Gary Bauer, *Children at Risk: The Battle for the Hearts and Minds of Our Kids* (Dallas: Word, 1990), 23.

24. Ibid., 33.

25. Ibid.

Chapter 2

1. Arlene Skolnick, *Embattled Paradise: The American Family in*

an Age of Uncertainty (New York: HarperCollins, Basic Books, 1991), 225.

2. U.S. Bureau of the Census, Current Population Reports P23-181, *Households, Families, and Children: A Thirty Year Perspective* (Washington, D.C.: U.S. Government Printing Office, 1992), 8.

3. Dennis A. Ahlburg and Carol J. De Vita, "New Realities of the American Family," *Population Bulletin* 47, no. 2 (August 1992): 12.

4. U.S. Bureau of the Census, *Households, Families and Children*, 6.

5. Ahlburg and De Vita, "New Realities," 12.

6. Larry L. Bumpass, James A. Sweet, and Andrew Cherlin, "The Role of Cohabitation in Declining Rates of Marriage," *Journal of Marriage and the Family* 53, no. 4 (November 1991): 913-27.

7. Newsletter of the International Anglican Family Network.

8. William Julius Wilson, *The Truly Disadvantaged: The Inner City, the Underclass, and Public Policy* (Chicago: University of Chicago Press, 1987).

9. Ahlburg and De Vita, "New Realities," 17.

10. The Council on Families in America, *Marriage in America: A Report to the Nation* (Washington, D.C.: Institute for American Values, 1995).

11. Ibid.

12. Ahlburg and De Vita, "New Realities," 5.

13. Ibid., 7.

14. Larry L. Bumpass, "What's Happening to the Family? Interactions between Demographic Institutional Change: Presidential Address, Annual Meeting of the Population Association of America," *Demography* 27: 483-98.

15. Jerry M. Lewis and John Looney, *The Long Struggle: Well-Functioning Working Class Black Families* (New York: Bruner/Mazel, 1983).

16. For the most recent statistical information on children and poverty, consult the annual *State of the Child* report of the Children's Defense Fund, available from 25 E Street NW, Washington, DC 20001. See also *Beyond Rhetoric: A New American Agenda for Children and Families*, the final report of the National Commission on Children (Washington, D.C.: U.S. Government Printing Office).

17. The study was conducted by Martha Burt of the Urban Institute. See Martha R. Burt, *Over the Edge: The Growth of Homelessness in the 1980s* (New York: Russell Sage Foundation, 1992).

18. Periodic surveys of domestic violence are done by the U. S. Justice Department and by the National Institutes of Mental Health. For an up-to-date discussion see Ann Jones, *Next Time She'll Be Dead: Battering and How to Stop It* (Boston: Beacon Press, 1994).

19. U.S. Bureau of the Census, *Households, Families and Children,* 28.

20. Peter Bailey, ed., *At-Home Dad* 1 (Spring 1994). Available at 61 Brightwood Ave., North Andover, MA 01845.

21. The information in the three paragraphs that follow the noted paragraph is taken from the publications of two futurists: David Pearce Snyder, *The Family in Trans-Industrial America* (Bethesda, Md.: E-S Press, 1991); Gregg Edwards and David Pearce Snyder, *Families Forge the Future: Sustaining the Social Base of Our Economic Enterprise* (Bethesda, Md.: E-S Press, 1993).

22. Marilyn Hoffman, "Renovation Business Booming," *Washington Post,* October 9, 1982.

23. For information about the Parenting for Peace and Justice Network (PPJN), write them at the Institute for Peace and Justice, 4144 Lindell Blvd. Suite 124, St. Louis, MO 63108. For an introduction to the concepts of parenting for peace and justice, see Kathleen McGinnis and James McGinnis, *Parenting for Peace and Justice: Ten Years Later* (Maryknoll, N.Y.: Orbis, 1990).

24. Karen Bernstine, ed., *Black Family Ministry Manual* (Valley Forge, Pa.: Judson, forthcoming 1996). This publication was produced by the Black Family Ministry Project of the Commission on Family Ministries and Human Sexuality, National Council of the Churches of Christ in the USA and funded in part by the Lilly Endowment.

Chapter 3

1. Willie S. Teague, "What Is a Christian Family?" *Weavings* 3, no. 1 (January–February 1988): 27, 31.

2. H. Richard Niebuhr, *Christ and Culture* (New York: Harper & Brothers, 1951).

3. Virginia Ramey Mollenkott, *Sensuous Spirituality: Out from Fundamentalism* (New York: Crossroad, 1992), 194-97.

4. Paul Eppinger, "A Theology of Divorce," in *Single Adults—The*

Exploding Ministry of the '80s (Topeka: First Baptist Church of Topeka, nd), 2-12.

5. Rodney Clapp, *Families at the Crossroads* (Downers Grove, Ill.: InterVarsity Press, 1993), 35-37.

6. Myrna Kysar and Robert Kysar, *The Asundered: Biblical Teachings on Divorce and Remarriage* (Atlanta: John Knox Press, 1978), 56-57.

7. Richard J. Foster, *Money, Sex, and Power: The Challenge of the Disciplined Life* (San Francisco: Harper & Row, 1985), 148.

8. Clapp, *Families at the Crossroads,* 113.

9. Isabel W. Rogers, "Healthy Families: Fact and Faith," *Church and Society* 84, no. 2 (November–December 1993): 60–61.

10. Janet Fishburn, *Confronting the Idolatry of the Family: A New Vision for the Household of God* (Nashville: Abingdon Press, 1991), 11, 84, 183.

11. Clapp, *Families at the Crossroads,* 67–68.

12. Peter Lampe, "The Family of New Testament Times," *Church and Society* 84, no. 2 (November-December 1993): 29.

13. Ibid., 30.

Chapter 4

1. Diana Garland, "Strengthening Families and Churches in Turbulent Times," *Journal of Family Ministry* 9, no. 1 (1995): 5-21.

2. Elise Boulding, "Familia Faber: The Family as Maker of the Future," *Journal of Marriage and the Family* 45: 257-66.

3. For a discussion of the concept of family support and guidelines for its practice in human service settings, see Carl Dunst, Carol Trivette, and Angela Deal, *Enabling and Empowering Families: Principles and Guidelines for Practice* (Cambridge, Mass.: Brookline Books, 1988).

4. See Peter L. Benson, *The Troubled Journey: A Portrait of 6th-12th Grade Youth* (Minneapolis: Search Institute, 1990). A study of outcomes for youth in single-parent families based on the same data is reported in Peter L. Benson and Eugene C. Roehlkepartain, *Youth in Single-Parent Families: Risk and Resiliency* (Minneapolis: Search Institute, 1993). Communitywide strategies for improving outcomes among youth are outlined in Dale A. Blyth and Eugene C. Roehlkepartain, *Healthy*

Communities, Healthy Youth: How Communities Contribute to Positive Youth Development (Minneapolis: Search Institute, 1993); includes "Implications for Religious Leaders."

5. For information, contact the Interfaith Hospitality Networks for the Homeless, 120 Morris Ave., Summit, NJ 07901.

6. Rodney Clapp, *Families at the Crossroads* (Downers Grove, Ill.: InterVarsity Press, 1993), 162-63.

7. James and Kathleen McGinnis, *Parenting for Peace and Justice: Ten Years Later* (Maryknoll, N.Y.: Orbis, 1990).

8. Garland, "Strengthening Families and Churches," 10.

9. For information, write Parenting for Peace and Justice, c/o The Institute for Peace and Justice, 4144 Lindell Blvd. #124, St. Louis, MO 63108.

10. Virginia Satir, *Conjoint Family Therapy* (Palo Alto, Calif.: Science and Behavior Books, 1964); *The New Peoplemaking* (Palo Alto, Calif: Science and Behavior Books, 1988). Summarized in Froma Walsh, ed., *Normal Family Processes*, 2nd ed. (New York: Guilford Press, 1993).

11. Froma Walsh, ed., *Normal Family Processes*, 2nd ed. (New York: Guilford Press, 1993), 58-59.

12. Jack Mezirow, "Perspective Transformation," *Studies in Adult Education* 9 (1977): 153-64.

13. Margaret Sawin, *Family Enrichment with Family Clusters* (Valley Forge, Pa.: Judson Press, 1979).

14. See Joe H. Leonard, Jr., *Family: Where the Generations Meet* (Louisville: Presbyterian Publishing House, 1994); or write for a catalog of resources: Carolyn and Larry Gabbard, Executive Director, Presbyterian Mariners, 11555 W. 78th Dr., Arvada, CO 80005.

15. Blyth and Roehlkepartain, *Healthy Communities, Healthy Youth*, 35.

16. Diana Garland, et al., eds., *Life-Changing Events for Youth and Their Families* (Nashville: Convention Press, 1995).

17. Jeanette Lauer and Robert Lauer, "Marriages Made to Last," *Psychology Today* 19, no. 6 (June 1985): 22-26.

18. David H. Olson (Prepare/Enrich, Inc.,1992).

19. David and Vera Mace, *We Can Have Better Marriages* (Nashville: Abingdon Press, 1973).

20. This strategy is discussed in Michael McManus, *Marriage*

Savers: Helping Your Friends and Family Stay Married (Grand Rapids: Zondervan, 1993), 199-212.

21. Carolyn Koons and Michael Anthony, *Single Adult Passages: Uncharted Territories* (Grand Rapids: Baker, 1991), 17-19.

22. Kay Collier-Slone, *Single in the Church* (Bethesda, Md.: The Alban Institute, 1992).

Chapter 5

1. Jean Bethke Elshtain, "On the Family Crisis," *Democracy* 3 (Winter 1983).

2. Don S. Browning and Carol Browning, "The Church and the Family Crisis: A New Love Ethic," *Christian Century*, August 7-14, 1991: 747.

3. Betty Vos, "Practicing a Love Ethic for All Families," *Christian Century*, November 18, 1991: 1060–61.

4. Tim Emerick-Cayton, *Divorcing with Dignity (Mediation: The Sensible Alternative)* (Louisville: Westminster/John Knox Press, 1993), 75.

5. Ibid., 1.

6. Emily B. Visher and John S. Visher, *Old Loyalties, New Ties: Therapeutic Strategies with Stepfamilies* (New York: Brunner/Mazel, 1988), ix.

7. Ibid., 10.

8. Ibid., 3.

9. Ibid., 6.

10. George Barna, *The Future of the American Family* (Chicago: Moody Press, 1993), 182.

11. Jean Curtis, *Working Mothers* (Garden City, N.Y.: Doubleday, 1976), 57ff.

12. Hyman Rodman, "From Latchkey Stereotypes toward Self Care Realities," in *Family and Support Systems across the Life Span,* ed. Suzanne K. Steinmetz (New York: Plenum Press, 1988), 99-104.

13. Bonnie Michaels and Elizabeth McCarty, *Solving the Work Family Puzzle* (Homewood, Ill.: Managing Work and Family, 1992). For information about Work/Family Retreats, contact Bonnie Michaels at Managing Work and Family, Inc., 912 Crain, Evanston, IL 90202.

14. For many insights we are indebted to the fine ethical work of Marie M. Fortune, *Love Does No Harm: Sexual Ethics for the Rest of Us* (New York: Continuum, 1995).

15. Ibid., 79.

16. Ibid., 115.

17. Judy Root Aulette, *Changing Families* (Belmont, Calif.: Wadsworth, 1994), 358-61.

18. Kristin Luker, "Dubious Conceptions: The Controversy Over Teen Pregnancy," in *Family in Transition: Rethinking Marriage, Sexuality, Child Rearing, and Family Organization*, ed. Arlene S. Skolnick and Jerome H. Skolnick, 7th ed. (New York: HarperCollins, 1992), 172.

19. Marian Wright Edelman, *Families in Peril: An Agenda For Social Change* (Cambridge, Mass.: Harvard University Press, 1987), 58, 64-66.

20. See the provocative and disturbing discussion of what is happening to young girls in school and in our culture in Mary Pipher, *Reviving Ophelia: Saving the Selves of Adolescent Girls* (New York: Ballantine, 1994).

21. See ch. 1, subhead "An Extended and Sometimes Troubled Adolescence." See also Marie M. Fortune, *Love Does No Harm: Sexual Ethics for the Rest of Us* (New York: Continuum, 1995), ch. 6.

22. Michael McManus, *Marriage Savers: Helping Your Friends and Family Stay Married* (Grand Rapids: Zondervan, 1994).

23. Robert Schoen, "First Unions and the Stability of First Marriages," *Journal of Marriage and the Family* 54, no. 2 (May 1992): 281-84.

24. Alfred DeMaris and William MacDonald, "Premarital Cohabitation and Marital Instability: A Test of the Unconventionality Hypothesis," *Journal of Marriage and the Family* 55, no. 2 (May 1993): 399-407.

25. Mary Beekley-Peacock, "Making a Commitment," in the Family Week 1995 Packet "Strengthening Families for Change: Making Commitments—Living Them Out" (New York: Commission on Family Ministries and Human Sexuality of the National Council of Churches, 1995).

26. Tom Koch, *Mirrored Lives: Aging Children and Elderly Parents* (New York: Praeger, 1990), 189-99.

RESOURCES

Basic Information

Ahlburg, Dennis A. and Carol J. De Vita. "New Realities of the American Family." *Population Bulletin*, Vol.47, No. 2. Washington, DC: Population Reference Bureau, Inc., August 1992.

Aulette, Judy Root. *Changing Families*. Belmont, CA: Wadsworth Publishing Company, 1994.

Barna, George. *The Future of the American Family*. Chicago: Moody Press, 1993.

Benson, Peter L. *The Troubled Journey: A portrait of 6th-12th grade youth*. Minneapolis, MN: Search Institute, 1990.

_____ and Eugene C. Roehlkepartain. *Youth in Single-Parent Families: Risk and Resiliency*. Minneapolis, MN: Search Institute, 1993.

Burt, Martha R. *Over the Edge: The Growth of Homelessness in the 1980s*. New York: Russell Sage Foundation, 1992.

Coontz, Stephanie. *The Way We Never Were: American Families and the Nostalgia Trap*. New York: Basic Books, a Division of Harper Collins Publishers, 1992.

Dunst, Carl, Carol Trivette, and Angela Deal. *Enabling and Empowering Families: Principles and Guidelines for Practice*. Cambridge, MA: Brookline Books, 1988.

Jones, Ann. *Next Time She'll Be Dead: Battering and How to Stop It*. Boston: Beacon Press, 1994.

Lewis, Jerry M. and John Looney. *The Long Struggle: Well-Functioning Working Class Black Families*. New York: Bruner/Mazel, 1983.

Satir, Virginia. *The New Peoplemaking*. Palo Alto, CA: Science and
     Behavior Books, 1988.

Skolnick, Arlene. *Embattled Paradise: The American Family in an Age
     of Uncertainty*. New York: Basic Books, a Division of Harper
     Collins Publishers, 1991.

Smith, Wallace Charles. *The Church in the Life of the Black Family*.
     Valley Forge, PA: Judson Press, 1985.

Walsh, Froma, ed. *Normal Family Processes*, 2nd ed. New York: The
     Guilford Press, 1993.

Programmatic Resources

Bernstine, Karen, ed. *Black Family Ministry Manual*. Valley Forge, PA:
     Judson Press, 1996.

Blyth, Dale A. and Eugene C. Roehlkepartain. *Healthy Communities,
     Healthy Youth: How Communities Contribute to Positive Youth
     Development*. Minneapolis, MN: Search Institute, 1993.

Carlson, Lee W., ed. *Christian Parenting: Resources for Group Use*.
     Valley Forge, PA: Judson Press, 1985.

Crohn, Joel. *Mixed Matches: How to Create Successful Interracial,
     Interethnic, and Interfaith Relationships*. New York: Fawcett
     Columbine, 1995.

Farnham, Suzanne et. al. *Listening Hearts: Discerning Call in Commu-
     nity*. Harrisburg, PA: Morehouse 1991.

Fortune, Marie M. *Sexual Abuse Prevention: A Study for Teenagers*.
     New York: United Church Press, 1984.

_____ . *Violence in the Family: A Workshop Curriculum for
     Clergy and Other Helpers*. Cleveland, OH: The Pilgrim Press, 1991.

Garland, Diana, Richard Ross, Lese Chandler, and Wade Rowatt, eds.
     Life-Changing Events for Youth and their Families. Nashville, TN:
     Convention Press, 1995.

Green, Tova, Fran Peavy, and Peter Woodrow. *Insight and Action*
     Philadelphia, PA: New Society Press, 1994.

Harris, Frank W. *Great Games to Play with Groups*. Carthage IL:
     Fearon Teacher Aids, 1989.

Koch, Tom. *Mirrored Lives: Aging Children and Elderly Parents*. New
     York: Praeger, 1990.

Leonard, Joe H. Jr. *Family: Where the Generations Meet.* Louisville, KY: Presbyterian Publishing House, 1994 or write Carolyn and Larry Gabbard, Executive Director, Presbyterian Mariners, 11555 West 78th Drive, Arvada, CO 80005.

Loring, Patricia. *Spiritual Discernment: The Context and Goal of Clearness Committees.* Pendle Hill Pamphlet 305 (Pendle Hill PA: Pendel Hill Pamphlets, 1992).

McGinnis, James and Kathleen McGinnis. *Parenting for Peace and Justice, Ten Years Later.* Maryknoll, NY: Orbis Books, 1990.

McManus, Michael J. *Marriage Savers: Helping Your Friends and Family Stay Married.* Grand Rapids, MI: Zondervan Publishing House, 1993.

Michaels, Bonnie and Elizabeth McCarty. *Solving the Work Family Puzzle.* Homewood, IL: Managing Work & Family, Inc., 1992.

Orlik, Terry. *The Cooperative Sports and Games Book: Challenge Without Competition.* New York: Pantheon Books, 1978.

Popkin, Michael H. and David Englestad. *Active Christian Parenting.* Marietta, GA: Active Parenting Publishers and Minneapolis; MN: Augsburg Fortress, 1995.

Reid, Kathryn Goering and Marie Fortune. *Preventing Child Sexual Abuse: A Curriculum for Children Ages 9-12.* New York: United Church Press, 1989); see also companion volume by Kathryn Goering Reid, *Preventing Child Sexual Abuse: A Curriculum for Children Ages 5-8.* Cleveland, OH: United Church Press, 1995.

Visher, Emily B. and John S. Visher. *Old Loyalties, New Ties: Therapeutic Strategies with Stepfamilies.* New York: Brunner/Mazel Publishers, 1988.

Weinstein, Matt and Goodman, Joel. *Play Fair: Everybody's Guide to Non-Competitive Play.* San Luis Obispo, CA: Impact Publishers, 1980.

Theological Perspectives

Clapp, Rodney. *Families at the Crossroads.* Downers Grove, IL: Intervarsity Press, 1993.

Dobson, James and Gary Bauer. *Children At Risk: The Battle for the Hearts and Minds of Our Kids.* Dallas: Word Publishing, 1990.

Fishburn, Janet. *Confronting the Idolatry of the Family: A New Vision for the Household of God.* Nashville: Abingdon Press, 1991.

Fortune, Marie. *Love Does No Harm: Sexual Ethics for the Rest of Us.* New York: Continuum, 1995.

Koons, Carolyn A. and Michael J. Anthony. *Single Adult Passages: Uncharted Territories.* Grand Rapids, MI: Baker Book House, 1991.

Kysar, Myrna and Robert Kysar. *The Asundered: Biblical Teachings on Divorce and Remarriage.* Atlanta: John Knox Press, 1978.

Mollenkott, Virginia Ramsey. *Sensuous Spirituality: Out From Fundamentalism.* New York: Crossroad, 1992.

New England Yearly Meeting. *Living with Oneself and Others: Working Papers on Aspects of Family Life.* (Order from Friends General Conference Bookstore, 1216 Arch Street 2-B, Philadelphia 19107. Telephone: 1-800-966-4556.)

Olson, Richard P. and Joe H. Leonard, Jr. *Ministry with Families in Flux: The Church and Changing Patterns of Life.* Louisville: Westminster/John Knox, 1990.

Sociological and Psychological Perspectives

Edelman, Marian Wright. *Families in Peril: An Agenda For Social Change.* Cambridge, MA: Harvard University Press, 1987.

Emerick-Cayton, Tim. *Divorcing with Dignity. (Mediation: The Sensible Alternative).* Louisville: Westminster/John Knox Press, 1993.

Hechinger, Fred M. *Fateful Choices: Healthy Youth for the Twenty First Century.* New York: Hill and Wang, a Division of Farrar, Straus, and Giroux, 1992.

Pipher, Mary. *Reviving Ophelia: Saving the Selves of Adolescent Girls.* New York: Ballantine Books, 1994.

Skolnick, Arlene S., and Jerome H. Skolnick. *Family In Transition: Rethinking Marriage, Sexuality, Child Rearing, and Family Organization,* 7th ed. Harper Collins Publishers, 1992.

Steinmetz, Suzanne K. ed. *Family And Support Systems Across The Life Span.* New York: Plenum Press, 1988)

Zinn, Maxine Baca and D. Stanley Eitzen. *Diversity in Families.* New York: Harper and Row, 1990.

Organizations

Active Parenting is a secular organization that produces video-based parent-training materials and offers workshops to train instructors. They have also co-published *Active Christian Parenting* by Michael H. Popkin and David Englestad. Marietta, GA: Active Parenting Publishers and Minneapolis, MN: Augsburg Fortress, 1995. Contact Active Parenting Publishers, 810 Franklin Court Suite B, Marietta, GA 30067. Telephone: 1-800-825-0060.

Academy of Family Mediators, a professional organization which provides a national directory listing individuals who have completed certified training in mediation. Contact the Academy of Family Mediators at 4 Militia Drive, Lexington, MA 02173. Telephone: 617-674-2663.

Association of Couples in Marriage Enrichment (ACME) is an organization dedicated to building strong marriages through all forms of enrichment strategies. For information about retreats, leader couple training, and a directory of certified leaders, contact the Association at P. O. Box 10596, Winston-Salem, NC 27108. Telephone: 910-724-1526.

Association of Family and Conciliation Courts provides information about and advocates court-connected mediation. The Association also advocates for court associated and court mandated educational programs for separating/divorcing parents and for children whose parents are separating/divorcing. Contact the Association at 329 West Wilson Street, Madison, WI 53703-3612. Telephone: 608-251-4001.

At-Home Dad is a newsletter for and about fathers who are the full-time, primary care-givers of their children. For a sample issue or to subscribe, contact *At-Home Dad*, Peter Bailey, editor, 61 Brightwood Avenue, North Andover, MA 01845 or e-mail: athomedad@aol.com.

Center for Media Literacy is a non-profit membership organization dedicated to a media literate citizenry. The Center publishes a newsletter, Connect, conducts training workshops and is the largest producer of media literacy materials in North America. Contact the Center for Media Literacy at 1962 Shenandoah, Los Angeles, CA 90034. Telephone: 1-800-226-9494.

Center for the Prevention of Sexual and Domestic Violence, an interreligious educational agency, provides excellent videos for religious congregations and organizations on the nature and prevention of domestic violence, on preventing emotional, physical, and sexual child abuse, and on how congregations can educate members about these concerns. The Center offers training workshops for clergy, for seminaries, and for religious educators. They publish a newsletter. Founded and directed by the Reverend Marie M. Fortune, the Center is the foremost religious organization in the field of domestic violence and sexual abuse prevention. Contact the Center for the Prevention of Sexual and Domestic Violence at 936 North 34th Street, Suite 200, Seattle, WA 98103. Telephone: 206-634-1903.

Commission on Family Ministries and Human Sexuality, National Council of the Churches of Christ, is a coalition of twenty denominations and family-serving organizations. For information about resources for family ministries, sexuality education, and alternative rituals for recognizing family events, contact the Commission on family Ministries and Human Sexuality, National Council of the Churches of Christ, 475 Riverside Drive, Room 848, New York, NY10115-0050. Telephone: 212-870-2673.

Interfaith Hospitality Networks for the Homeless is a national association of local networks of congregations providing shelter, job counseling, child care, and parent education to homeless families in about half of the states of the US. In each locality, Jewish and Christian congregations link up to shelter and help homeless families find homes, jobs, and a better life. Many of the networks also do public education and advocacy on issues related to homelessness. Contact Interfaith Hospitality Networks for the Homeless at 120 Morris Avenue, Summit, NJ 07901.

Interpersonal Communication Programs, Inc. offers instructor training workshops and excellent resources in "Couple Communication." Their program teaches couples skills in self-awareness and disclosure, effective listening, conflict resolution, and communication styles. The effectiveness of both the methods of instruction and resources have been validated by careful research. For information about training workshops and a catalog, contact Interpersonal Communication Programs, Inc. at 7201 South Broadway #11, Littleton, CO 80122. Telephone: 303-794-1764.

International Exchange Programs: For a directory to programs, contact the Council on Standards for International Educational Travel, 3 Loudoun Street, SE, Suite 3, Leesburg, VA 22075.

Marriage Encounter is a lay led movement to strengthen marriages. Several "expressions" represented by several organizations exist:
- *Worldwide Marriage Encounter* began as a Catholic expression and serves as an umbrella for several denominationally specific marriage encounter organizations. Telephone: 1-800-795-LOVE.
- *International Marriage Encounter* pursues an ecumenical approach. Telephone: 1-800-828-3351.
- *United Marriage Encounter* is a Protestant oriented organization. Telephone: 1-800-634-8325.

Parenting for Peace and Justice Network offers training workshops and excellent parenting and intergenerational materials for use in Jewish, Catholic, and Protestant congregations. All resources and training are value-based and rooted in Scripture. The Network has international connections and offers opportunities for international exchange visits and study tours. Contact Parenting for Peace and Justice Network, c/o The Institute for Peace and Justice, 4144 Lindell Boulevard #124, St Louis, MO 63108.

Parents, Families and Friends of Lesbians and Gays, Inc. is a national organization with local chapters that offer support groups to parents and family members and advocacy on behalf of sexual minority people. For information about local chapters, resources, and newsletter contact Parents, Families and Friends of Lesbians and Gays, Inc., 1101 14th Street NW, Washington, DC 20005. Telephone: 202-638-4200.

Parents Without Partners is a national organization with local chapters that focus on support and socialization for single parents. A directory of local chapters is available from the national office. Contact Parents Without Partners, Inc., 401 North Michigan Avenue, Chicago, IL 60611. Telephone: 312-644-6610.

Prepare/Enrich, Inc. offers clergy counselors tools for helping couples identify strengths and growing edges in their relationships. Clergy and counselors are required to attend a one-day workshop which teaches them to administer, interpret and counsel using the Prepare/Enrich program. Contact Prepare/Enrich, Inc. at P. O. Box 190, Minneapolis, MN 55440-0190. Telephone: 1-800-331-1661.

Presbyterian Mariners is a couples and family organization in the Presbyterian Church USA. Contact Carolyn and Larry Gabbard, Executive Directors, 11555 West 78th Drive, Arvada, CO 80005.

Stepfamily Association of America is a national organization with local chapters that offer support, education, and activities for stepfamilies. They also provide resources for leaders of stepfamily groups. Contact Stepfamily Association of America, 28 Allegheny Avenue, Suite 1307, Baltimore, MD 21204.